366 readings from
TAOISM AND
CONFUCIANISM

THE GLOBAL SPIRIT LIBRARY

366 readings from
TAOISM AND CONFUCIANISM

edited by

ROBERT VAN DE WEYER

THE PILGRIM PRESS
CLEVELAND, OHIO

ARTHUR JAMES
NEW ALRESFORD, UK

First published in USA and Canada by
The Pilgrim Press,
700 Prospect Avenue East, Cleveland, Ohio 44115

First published in English outside North America by
Arthur James Ltd,
46a West Street, New Alresford, UK, SO24 9AU

North America ISBN 0-8298-1392-6
English language outside North America ISBN 0 85305 456 8

Typeset in Monotype Joanna by
Strathmore Publishing Services, London N7

Printed by
Tien Wah Press, Singapore

CONTENTS

SERIES INTRODUCTION

The Global Spirit Library is the first comprehensive collection of the spiritual literature of the world, presented in accessible form. It is aimed at people who belong to a particular religious community, and wish to broaden their spiritual outlook; and at the much larger group, perhaps the majority of people in the world today, who have little or no attachment to a religious community, but seek spiritual wisdom. Each book contains the major writings of one of the world's spiritual traditions.

Much of the world's spiritual literature was designed to be read or heard in small portions, allowing ample time for personal reflection. Following this custom, the books in *The Global Spirit Library* each consist of an annual cycle of daily readings. Two or more books may be read in parallel at different times of the day; or an entire book may be read straight through. Again following a time-honoured practice, many of the original texts have been condensed.

Spiritual traditions differ from one another in their theological formulations; and the history of humankind is blighted by rivalry between different religious communities. Yet theology is no more than human speculation about truths that are beyond the grasp of the human mind. The writings in these books amply demonstrate that, as men and women actually experience these truths within themselves and others, divisions and rivalries fade, and unity is found. May the third millennium be an era of spiritual unity across the globe.

INTRODUCTION

Tao is best translated as the 'Way'; it may also be understood as the first principle from which everything comes, and to which all will return. So a Taoist is someone who follows the Way, by seeking to live in accordance with the principle of existence.

No one knows when the term was first coined, or when its meaning began to be taught. But there were certainly Taoist sages from the middle of the first millennium BCE. For many centuries Taoism had no formal organization and no buildings; there were simply sages who attracted disciples, and whose actions and words were sometimes written down. By the fourth and third centuries BCE the advice of these sages was eagerly sought by kings and noblemen, and by humble craftsmen and farmers. Most of the great Taoist literature dates from this period. When Buddhism reached China, it was heavily influenced by Taoism; and Chan (known in Japan as Zen) may be regarded as a Taoist form of Buddhism. During the first millennium CE Taoism became more institutionalized, with sects, hierarchies and temples; and Taoist thinkers engaged in theological speculation that the earlier sages would have regarded as vain. But in the latter part of the second millennium the teachings of the sages gained new popularity in the West.

The teachings of Kung Fu Tzu (Confucius), and those of his greatest follower Meng Tzu (Mencius), are often contrasted with those of the great Taoist teachers. But in fact there is a large overlap, and the differences are complementary. Thus they are included in this volume.

TAO TE CHING

A collection of eighty-one short chapters, *Tao Te Ching* – which means 'Scripture of the Tao and its Power' – is the most famous of all Taoist works; and many later works presented themselves as commentaries on it. Traditionally it is attributed to Lao Tzu, living in the sixth century BCE. But there is considerable doubt as to whether he ever existed; and the work may be a compilation of the sayings of a number of philosophers. There is also doubt about the date, with some suggesting that the compilation may have been made in the fourth century BCE.

The hidden and the manifest

The way of which you can speak, is not the true Way. The name that can be uttered, is not the true Name.

Heaven and earth begin in the unnamed. Name is the mother of the numerous living beings.

In order to discern that which is hidden, you must rid yourself of all desire. But in order to see that which is manifest, you must be filled with desire.

The hidden and the manifest are one; they have a single origin. Yet they diverge as they come forth. Their sameness is a mystery, the mystery of all mysteries. The manifest is the gateway to the hidden.

1

A thing and its opposite

The fact that everyone on earth knows that beauty is beautiful, makes ugliness. The fact that everyone on earth knows that goodness is good, makes evil.

A thing and its opposite produce one another, and complement one another. Some things are called difficult, because other things are easy. The long and the short shape one another. The high and the low depend on each other. Sound and pitch together make music. Before and after follow one another.

Thus the wise person does deeds that consist in taking no action, and teaches others without talking.

The things of this world exist; they are; you cannot deny them.

The wise person owns, without possessing; does good, without expecting gratitude; performs tasks, without taking credit. Since wise people never take credit for what they do, they are honoured.

2

Empty minds and full bellies

If no one were to praise actions that are worthy of praise, then there would be no competition between people.

If no one were to value precious treasures, then there would be no stealing.

If no one desired that which is desirable, then people's minds would be tranquil and serene.

So if a wise person were ruler, he would empty the people's minds, fill their bellies, weaken their desires, and strengthen their bodies. He would strive to ensure people knew nothing and wanted nothing. And if certain people got to know something, he would prevent them from acting on their knowledge.

When you never seek to be honoured for what you do, then honour can never desert you.

Space like a bellows

The Way is empty, but it has not been drained. The Way has been used, but it has not been used up. It is deep; it is the ancestor of all living beings.

Blunt every sharp edge. Untangle every knot. Soften all that glares. Let your wheels move slowly along old ruts.

That which is quiet is likely to endure.

Heaven and earth are ruthless. They treat all living beings like straw dogs, to be discarded and trampled upon at will.

Is not the space between heaven and earth like a bellows? It is empty, and yet it is structured. It moves, and yet it does not change.

Wise speech points towards silence. Structure points towards emptiness. So it is better to lay hold of silence and emptiness.

4, 5

Leaving self behind

The spirit of a valley never dies. It is a mystery; and it is female. The gateway of this same mysterious female is the root of earth and heaven. It lasts forever, and it is always easy to use.

Heaven and earth will endure. The reason for this is that they do not exist for themselves; they do not give themselves life. Hence they can go on and on.

The wise person leaves self behind, and moves forward on the Way. The self is extraneous to human life; and by leaving it behind the wise person reaches the centre of life.

Why let the self go? Without letting go the self, the soul's needs cannot be met.

6, 7

Goodness like water

True goodness is like water. Since water benefits everything, it competes with nothing. It even finds its way to the lowest, most filthy places, and brings benefit.

In order to build a house, level ground is needed. In order to think well, depth is needed. In order for two people to be friends, mutual affection is needed. In order to speak well, honesty and sensitivity are needed. In order to have good government, order is needed. In order to perform a task well, the appropriate skill is needed. In order to succeed in any venture, the right timing is needed.

If people did not compare themselves with one another, they would not judge one another.

8

A little bluntness

Rather than fill a bowl to the brim, so that it spills over, it is better to leave a little space. Rather than sharpen a blade excessively, so that the blade easily breaks, it is better to leave a little bluntness.

Rather than fill your house with gold and jade, which tempt robbers to break in, it is better to have only simple furniture and ornaments.

Those who strive for wealth and status, bring ruin on themselves. Work well and do good, but ask for neither honour nor reward; then you will be truly blessed.

9

Leadership without rule

Can you keep the soul in your body? Can your body function in harmony with the soul? Can you learn to be whole?

Can you draw your energy back into yourself? Can you become supple? Can you learn to be a baby?

Can you keep deep water still and clear, so that it reflects without distortion? Can you love people as they are?

Can you manage things without exerting authority? Can you organize things by doing nothing?

Can you open and close the gates of heaven with ease? Can you enter and leave heaven, as a bird enters and leaves its nest?

Can you pierce the mystery of the universe? Can you know without knowing?

Can you bear a child, give birth to it and nourish it, without possessing it?

Can you act without taking credit for your actions?

Can you lead, and not rule? Leadership without rule is a mysterious form of power.

10

Making something useful

Thirty spokes meet at the hub. The hub where the wheel rotates, making the wheel useful, is not where the wheel is.

The potter hollows out the clay to make a bowl. The place where the clay is poured, making the bowl useful, is not where the bowl is.

The builders construct a room, leaving spaces for a door and windows. The things that let people and light enter a room, making the room useful, are not where the room is.

So that which makes something useful, lies not in the thing itself.

11

The inner eye

When we see all the colours together in the brightness of the sun, we are blinded. When we hear all the notes of the musical scale played together, we are deafened. When we taste every flavour together, the palate is dulled.

Riding and hunting make people's minds go crazy with excitement. When people strive with all their might to become rich, they tie their minds in knots.

If you are wise, you should watch with the inner eye, not the outer eye. Then you will know what to keep, and what to let go.

12

The ruler's body and the body politic

To be concerned about whether people look upon you with favour, or whether you are in disgrace, is to live in fear.

To take the body seriously, is to make suffering inevitable.

Why does concern with favour and disgrace imply living in fear? Favour corrupts you; you fear losing it, and yet you are convinced you do not deserve it.

Why does taking the body seriously make suffering inevitable? You suffer because you are a body; if you were not a body, you could not suffer.

A ruler may treat the welfare of his own body above the welfare of the body politic; that would make him unworthy of trust. A ruler who treats the body politic with as much care as he treats his own body, is worthy of trust.

13

Invisible, inaudible and intangible

What cannot be seen, is called invisible. What cannot be heard, is called inaudible. What cannot be touched, is called intangible.

That which is invisible, inaudible and intangible is one. You cannot differentiate one invisible, inaudible, intangible thing from another; there is perfect unity in invisibility, inaudibility and intangibility.

Nor can you say that above or below invisibility, inaudibility and intangibility is visibility, audibility and tangibility.

This oneness can never be named. It both is, and is not; it exists, and it does not exist. It is the form of the unformed; it is the image of no image.

It is the unthinkable thought. You may face it, yet it cannot be faced. You may follow it, but it has no end.

Hold fast to the Way that people of old times followed, in order to live in the present. If you remember the times of antiquity, you hold the thread of now.

14

Too deep to fathom

People who know the Way are observant, subtle, penetrating, and wise. Their wisdom is too deep for others to fathom.

I cannot explain such people, but only describe them with similes. They are cautious, as if they were wading across a river in winter. They are alert, as if they were afraid of their neighbours. They are polite and quiet, as if they were guests in someone else's house. They are elusive like ice that is melting. Their thoughts have no shape, like uncut wood. Their minds are empty, like a valley. Their attitudes are murky, like muddy water.

Who can be muddy, and yet also be clear? Who can be at rest, and yet also be active?

To follow the Way is to be fulfilled and happy, without fulfilment. To follow the Way is to grow old, and yet constantly be young.

15

Returning to the root

Do your utmost to be empty. Hold firmly to stillness.

Thousands of events are occurring at any moment. Observe events as they occur, and observe them pass. Nothing lasts. Events are like flowers: they bloom for a time, and then sink back into their roots.

Returning to the root is peace. Yes, peace consists in accepting what is, and knowing what endures. With that acceptance and knowledge you are wise. Without that acceptance and knowledge your life descends into chaos and ruin.

If you know what endures, you are generous, magnanimous, gracious, and serene. If you know what endures, you follow the Way, because the Way endures forever. The body will come to an end, but that is no cause for fear.

16

Leaders and people

The best leaders are hardly known to their people; they are shadowy figures in the eyes of those they rule. The next best leaders are those who are known and admired by their people. Below them come leaders who are feared by their people. And the worst leaders are those who are despised by their people.

If leaders do not trust their people, their people will not trust them; if they give no trust, they will receive none.

If leaders enable their people to live well, and do not fuss or boast of their achievements, then the people will take the credit for themselves, saying: 'We did that.'

17

Paradoxes in society

When grand ambitions come to nothing, benevolence and righteousness take their place.

When scholarship and intelligence are given undue respect, hypocrisy and pretence flourish.

When the members of a family bicker and quarrel, they may love one another deeply, and be immensely loyal; the parents may be devoted to their children, and the children may respect their parents.

When members of a society engage in heated debates about how that society should be organized, they are true patriots.

I 8

Raw silk and uncut wood

Do not strive to be holy. Forget trying to be wise. If you cast aside all aspirations towards holiness and wisdom, your relatives and friends will be greatly relieved.

Do not strive to be virtuous. Forget trying to be good. If you cast aside all aspirations towards virtue and goodness, you will remember what true human compassion is.

Do not strive to plan for the future. Forget trying to build up assets. If you cast aside all ambitions towards wealth and riches, thieves and cheats will leave you alone.

But even these three rules can be ignored. All that matters is that you appreciate raw silk and uncut wood. Need little and want less. Then you can forget the rules. Your life will be free of trouble.

Being old

How much difference is there between yes and no? What difference is there between good and bad?

That which people fear, should be feared. That which brings people to despair, should be dreaded.

People around me are cheerful, as if they were at a party, or playing in a garden in springtime. Yet here I sit, alone, inactive and unmoved; I am like a baby too young to smile.

I am forlorn, as if I had no home in which to live. Most people have plenty, but I am poor. Most people are intelligent, but I am foolish. Most people are bright, but I am dull.

Most people have answers to the great issues of religion and philosophy, but I have only questions. I am like a ship adrift on the open sea, far from any harbour.

Most people have important things to do, but I have nothing to do. Most people are skilled at their tasks, but I am clumsy.

I am odd. The only food I want is my mother's milk.

20

The nature of virtue

The virtue of any action lies in the extent to which it conforms to the Way. Virtue consists in following the Way, and only the Way.

It is hard to define the kind of action that conforms to the Way. Yes, such a definition is elusive; and even if it could be given, it would be hard to grasp.

Yet virtue is not beyond thought. And when it is practised, it can be recognized for what it is.

There is truth is virtue; you cannot be both virtuous and false. There is certainty in virtue; you cannot mistake virtue for something else. There is constancy in virtue; it has remained the same since the beginning of time.

Virtue has witnessed all history; it was present at the beginning. How do I know this? I know it by knowing the Way.

21

Being broken to be whole

In order to be whole, you must be broken. In order to be straight, you must be twisted. In order to be full, you must be empty. In order to be renewed, you must be worn out. In order to gain much, you must have little. In order to understand, you must be confused.

Wise people understand the unity of all things, and know that unity consists in diversity.

In order to be well known, you must never pursue fame. In order to be above suspicion, you must never justify yourself. In order to be honoured, you must never seek praise. In order to win, you must never compete.

Wise people in the past frequently said: 'In order to be whole, you must be broken.' Were they mistaken? It is certainly true that those who are broken, are most likely to flourish.

22

Being brief

It is natural to be sparing with words — to speak with brevity. A high wind rarely lasts all morning. A cloudburst rarely lasts all day. What makes the wind blow and the rain fall? Heaven and earth do. If heaven and earth are brief, then people should be brief also.

People of the Way follow the Way; they belong to the Way. People of virtue follow the path of virtue; they belong to virtue. People of simplicity are simple in all they do; they belong to simplicity.

Give yourself to the Way, and the Way will gladly accept you. Give yourself to virtue, and virtue will embrace you. Give yourself to simplicity, and simplicity will receive you with open arms.

If you do not trust, you will not be trusted.

23

Self-promotion

You cannot stand on tiptoe for long. If your stride is too great and your pace too fast, you will soon become exhausted.

If you boast and show off, people will not respect or admire you. If you try to advance your career by pushing others back, someone will eventually stop you. If you are satisfied with yourself, others will not be satisfied. If you speak eagerly of your own abilities, people will treat you as a bumptious child.

Self-promotion is to the Way, as poison is to food, or as a tumour is to the body. The Way hates self-promotion; so the follower of the Way avoids it.

24

Containing everything

There is an entity that contains everything. It existed before heaven and earth. It is unmoving and unchanging. It has no body or form. It is self-sufficient; it needs nothing apart from itself.

It pervades all that exists and all that happens. It is present in every object and every event. It is the mother and father of everything. We cannot know its true name; so we call it the Way.

If it must be named, let its name be 'Great'. This name signifies strength for the journey; strength for the journey enables the journey to be long; a long journey means that the destination will be reached, and there will be no turning back.

So we may say that the Way is great; heaven is great; earth is great; and humanity is great. There are four greatnesses, and humanity is one.

Human beings adapt themselves to the earth in which they live. Earth adapts itself to heaven, which has power over it. Heaven adapts itself to the Way, which contains everything. And the Way is that which eternally is.

25

Lightness and stillness

Lightness is rooted in heaviness; to be light of heart you must
have all the things that the body needs. Stillness is the master of moving; to move with grace and purpose, you must be
inwardly tranquil.

So when you are travelling all day, never let your luggage
out of your sight. Only when you have arrived safely in a
house that is solid and secure, can you lay anxiety aside.

A great king knows that his lightness of heart is rooted in
the well-being of his vast kingdom. His royal duties weigh
heavily on his mind; but if he were to lose that weight, his
heart would no longer be light.

A great king knows that his ability to move swiftly against
his enemies depends on his remaining calm and steady. He
may have ten thousand chariots behind him; but if he becomes so excited that he cannot give clear orders, they are
useless.

26

No tracks

Those who are fleet of foot, leave no tracks. Those who are eloquent, do not stumble over their words. Those who are good at arithmetic, do not use their fingers for counting.

The best door cannot be opened, except by those with the proper key. The best knot cannot be untied, except by those who know how to tie it.

Wise people are good at caring for others; they never turn away from anyone in need. Wise people are good at caring for animals and plants; they despise nothing that lives. They are guided by a hidden light.

Good people offer guidance to those who are less good. Less good people have the potential to be good.

Students who do not respect their teachers may be clever, but they will go astray. Teachers who do not cherish their students may be capable, but they have gone astray. Being capable and clever is not enough.

27

Female and male

The female should understand the male, yet not imitate him; she should be happy being female. The male should understand the female, yet not imitate her; he should be happy being male. Nothing can be built on a female foundation alone; and nothing can be built on a male foundation alone. But when the female and the male are together and yet distinct, the whole world can be built on them.

Darkness should understand light, yet not imitate it; darkness should be happy being dark. Light should understand dark, yet not imitate it; light should be happy being light. Nothing can be revealed by darkness alone; and nothing can be revealed by lightness alone. But when darkness and light are together and yet distinct, the mystery of eternity and infinity is made plain.

Glory should understand modesty, yet not imitate it; glory should be happy being glorious. Modesty should understand glory, yet not imitate it. Nothing can be gained by glory alone; and nothing can be gained by modesty alone. But when glory and modesty are together and yet distinct, the world can be made as it should be.

Uncut wood is carved to make useful things; wise people can be shaped into great leaders. The best carving is done without cutting and joining.

28

The world as sacred

Some people want to win the world by changing it; they always come to grief. The world is a sacred object. Nothing should be done to change it; any attempt to change it is bound to damage it. To try and possess the world, and treat it as your own, is to lose it.

Under heaven some people lead, and some follow. Some are gentle, and some are hard. Some are hot with passion, and some are cool. Some are strong, and some are weak. Some succeed in what they do, and some fail.

Wise people steer a middle course between extremes. They can lead or follow, as circumstances require. They can be gentle or hard, as circumstances require. They can be hot or cool, as circumstances require. They can be strong or weak, as circumstances require. And they make no distinction between success and failure.

29

Against war

A wise advisor restrains a ruler from trying to expand his rule through conquest. That tactic always rebounds onto the ruler himself.

In places over which armies have trampled, thorns and thistles grow. In the aftermath of battle the harvests are poor.

Good rulers want their people to be prosperous, not victorious. They want their people to enjoy comfort through honest toil, not glory through the slaughter of others. Glory never lasts; it flourishes for a while, and then fades. All things that are contrary to the Way are fleeting.

Even the finest weapon is a tool of misery and grief; so the follower of the Way avoids all weapons. Weapons are miserable tools spurned by the wise. They should be used only in extreme circumstances where there is no alternative – with a calm, clear mind, and without enjoyment. To enjoy using weapons, is to enjoy killing people; and to enjoy killing people is to take pleasure in the suffering of others.

The murder of people in war should be mourned. The victor in war should be received with funeral ceremonies.

30, 31

A stream to a valley

The Way is forever nameless; it can never have a title. It is
like a piece of uncut wood, that seems unimportant; yet nobody under heaven dares to carve it. If rulers and leaders
knew how to use it, tens of thousands of living beings would
come to pay them homage; heaven and earth would cover
their faces with the sweetest, softest dew; and their people,
without the need of laws, would be honest and kind to one
another.

When a ruler departs from the Way, he starts conferring
titles on his wealthier and more powerful subjects, to secure
their loyalty. When titles proliferate, it is a sign of weakness
and corruption. When a ruler feels no need or inclination to
confer titles, it is a sign of strength and justice.

The Way is to the world as a stream is to a valley, and a
river to a sea.

32

Intelligence and wisdom

If you know how other people behave, you are intelligent. If you know yourself, you are wise.

If you are able to overcome other people, you are strong. If you can overcome yourself, you are stronger.

If you are content with your circumstances, you are fortunate. If you are content with yourself, you are rich.

If you persevere in the face of adversity, you have determination. If you remain unmoved in the face of temptation or pressure, you have courage.

If you are happy to live until you die, then you will live as long as you want.

33

The greatness of the Way

The Way is broad; you can move far to the right and to the left, and still remain within it. Millions of living beings live on it, depend upon it for their existence; it accepts them willingly, and claims no authority over them.

The Way accomplishes its tasks, and claims no credit. It clothes and feeds the living beings who live on it; yet it imposes no obligations on them, and expects no gratitude from them.

The Way desires nothing, so it may be called small. Yet since it claims no credit, imposes no obligations, and expects no gratitude, it should be called great.

Wise people achieve greatness without doing great things.

34

Dull and insipid

If you are large-minded and open-hearted, the whole world belongs to you. You will not be in conflict with other living beings, but live in peace; your life will be serene.

When you walk around a town, you stop in one place to listen to stirring music, and in another to eat delicious food. If you listen to the Way, it seems dull; if you taste the Way, it seems insipid. Yet you cannot get enough of it.

That which shrinks, must first have grown. That which grows weak, must once have been strong. That which falls into a ruin, must once have been built. That which is given, must once have been taken.

If you are subtle in your perceptions, you know that those who are gentle and weak prevail over those who are harsh and strong.

35, 36

Nameless and natural

The Way never does anything; yet it leaves nothing undone.

If rulers and leaders followed the Way, and never deviated from it, their people would look after themselves. If I were advisor to a ruler, and the ruler tried to act, I should strive to calm him; I should urge him to return to that which is nameless and natural.

In that which has no name and no shape, there is freedom from desire. In freedom from desire there is stillness. In stillness all living beings under heaven are at rest.

37

Great power

Great power consists in not clinging to power; true power consists in not wanting power. People wanting power and clinging to power show their weakness.

Exerting great power consists in doing nothing; exerting true power consists in having nothing to do. Weak people are constantly striving to achieve something.

If weak people do nothing, they have some purpose in mind. If powerful people do nothing, they are inactive for its own sake.

Some people profess to live by high moral standards. Such people are constantly trying to make others conform to those standards – and sometimes use force to this end.

When we seek power, we lose the Way. When we lose power, we find the Way. But beware of taking pride in finding the Way, for fear that you will start claiming to live by high moral standards – and then lose the Way again.

Obedience to moral laws is the husk of truth; it is like a barren blossom that will not turn to fruit; it is ignorance appearing as goodness. People with great minds want the kernel, not the husk; they want the fruit, not the flower. They push moral laws aside, as rocks along the Way.

Following and deviating

Through following the Way, heaven is pure. Through following the Way, the earth is steady. Through following the Way, human beings are fulfilled. Through following the Way, the valley has a river running through it. Through following the Way, animals and insects thrive. Through following the Way, rulers have true power.

Following the Way makes that which is, become what it should be.

If heaven deviated from the Way, it would fall apart. If earth deviated from the Way, it would crumble. If humans deviate from the Way, they do not fulfil themselves. If the valley deviated from the Way, the river would run dry. If animals and insects deviate from the Way, they cease to thrive. If rulers deviate from the Way, they become weak.

The root of the nobleman is among the common people. That which is high stands on what is below. Kings and princes refer to themselves from time to time as solitary, desolate and hapless; in those words they expose their roots among their subjects.

Excessive wealth makes a person poor. Jade is called precious, but its hardness comes from being stone.

Jokes about the Way

Weakness is the strength by which you move along the Way. Turning back is the means by which you move forward.

The millions of living beings in the world are born of something. And something is born of nothing.

Wise people hear about the Way, and try hard to follow it. Ordinary people hear about the Way, and wander on and off it. Foolish people hear about the Way, and make jokes about it. After all, if the Way were not funny, it would not be the Way.

People say that the Way's brightness looks like darkness; that advancing along the Way feels like retreating; that the Way is so soft that walking along it is hard.

People say that the height of power seems as low as a deep valley; that the amplest power seems not enough; that the firmest power seems feeble. They say that pure virtue looks dirty; that unflagging vigour seems indolent.

People say that a square has no corners; that the finest musical note cannot be heard; that the most beautiful image has no shape.

The Way is hidden, so it has no name. But only the Way can bring you into existence, sustain you, and fulfil you.

40, 41

The blending of yin and yang

The Way bears one; one bears two; two bear three; and three bear the millions of living beings on earth. The millions of living beings carry the yin on their shoulders, and hold the yang in their arms. The blending of the yin energy and the yang energy creates harmony.

There are no words that people detest more than 'solitary', 'desolate', and 'hapless'. Yet kings and rulers frequently refer to themselves in these terms. Whatever you lose, you have won. Whatever you win, you have lost.

That which others teach, I also say: that violence and aggression destroy themselves. That is the summary of my teaching.

42

Water and stone

Water, which is the softest and most pliant substance in the world, flows over rock, which is the hardest and most rigid substance. And as it flows, it enters even the tiniest crevices. In the same way, the spiritual flows over the material, and penetrates it.

That is why I know the benefit of not resorting to action. I know the value of teaching that uses no words, and the profit in life that has no movement. Yet few in the world share my understanding.

Which is dearer to you, your name or your body? Which is worth more to you, your body or your wealth? Which gives you more pain, loss or gain?

That which you grasp, will be taken away from you. That which you hoard, will decay and rot.

Contentment is the best antidote to disgrace. Restraint is the best protection against danger. Contentment and restraint will sustain you for a long time.

43, 44

Knowing enough

That which is perfectly whole, seems flawed; yet you can use it forever. That which is perfectly full, seems empty; yet you can never drain it. That which is perfectly straight, appears crooked. That which is done with perfect skill and dexterity, seems clumsy. That which is expressed with perfect eloquence, seems confused.

To be comfortable in the cold, keep moving. To be comfortable in the heat, keep still. To be comfortable in the world, keep calm and clear.

When the world is following the Way, people use horses to plough and manure the fields. When the world has abandoned the Way, people use horses on the field of battle.

The greatest evil is to want more. The worst misfortune is discontent. The most terrible curse is greed.

If you know when enough is enough, you know enough.

45, 46

The place of inaction

You do not need to leave your house in order to know what happens in the world. You do not need to look out of the window to see the path to heaven. The further you travel, the less you understand.

Wise people do not move about, yet they know; they do not look, but they see; they do not act, but they do what needs to be done.

If you study books and memorize facts, you learn more day by day. If you follow the Way, you do less day by day. Eventually by following the Way you arrive at the place of inaction; in that place nothing is done, and nothing is undone.

To manage an organization well, do not fuss over it. Anyone who fusses, is unfit to manage anything.

47, 48

Good and faithful

If you are wise, you have no mind of your own; you find what is in the minds of the common people, and make it your own.

If you are wise, you are good to good people, and good to bad people. By this means you become good. If you are wise, you have faith in people of good faith, and you have faith in people of bad faith. By this means you become faithful.

If you are wise, you distrust order, and prefer muddle; so you take every opportunity to cause muddle. Ordinary people look after wise people; they regard wise people as children.

To look for life is to find death. The organs of the body that keep you alive, will eventually cause you to die. The means of life become the means of death. Do not cling too hard to life.

If you follow the Way, you can undertake any journey, and be certain of not meeting a mad bull or a tiger. If you follow the Way, no sword can slay you. The bull would find nowhere to jab his horns; the tiger would find nowhere to stick his claws; and a sword would have nowhere to pierce. Why? Because if you follow the Way, there is nowhere for death to enter.

49, 50

The mother of everything

The Way gives life to all living beings. Their parents nurture them. Their own inner energy shapes them. Their circumstances bring them to maturity. Every single living being holds the Way sacred, and submits to its authority. Their reverence for the Way, and their obedience to its authority, are natural and unforced.

To have without possessing, to do without claiming credit, to lead without controlling – these are the mysterious virtues of the Way.

The world had a beginning; and its beginning is the mother of everything. To know the mother is to know the children; and to know the children is to hold fast to the mother. And if you hold fast to the mother, then you have nothing to fear from bodily decay and death.

Close the door of achievement, and shut the window of cleverness; then in old age nothing will trouble you. Open the door to achievement, making yourself constantly busy, then in old age you will be irritable and unhappy.

If you have true knowledge, you know how to be ignorant. If you are truly strong, you have the strength to be weak. If you move by the light of the Way, your movement takes you nowhere.

At the centre of the wheel there is stillness.

51, 52

Teaching the world

If my mind is modest, I shall walk on the Way. If my mind is arrogant, I shall walk in fear. The Way is long, going round many mountains. But people prefer short cuts over the mountains.

Look at the splendid palaces in the world. The people within them are dressed in the finest robes, and decorated with sparkling jewels. They carry weapons to protect their wealth. They drink great quantities of wine, and eat vast meals. They have everything they want, and have gold with which to purchase whatever appeals to them. Yet they are shameless thieves; outside their gates the people are starving, and their granaries are empty. The way of life in a palace is not the Way.

A tree with firm roots cannot be pulled up. An object treasured by its owner will not be lost. The respect in which people hold their ancestors will never cease.

To follow the Way yourself is true virtue. To guide your family to follow the Way is greater virtue. To inspire your community to follow the Way is ample virtue. To lead a whole nation in following the Way is abundant virtue. To teach the whole world to follow the Way is untold virtue.

In myself I see what self is. In my home I see what family is. Amongst my neighbours I see what community is. In my country I see what nation is. In the world I see everything under heaven. How do I see the world? By staying here.

53, 54

A new-born baby

A person possessing virtue in abundance is like a new-born baby. Scorpions do not sting a baby; tigers do not pounce on it; eagles do not strike it. Its bones are soft and its sinews supple, but its grasp is firm. It knows nothing of the sexual attraction between a man and a woman, but its penis is erect. What energy it possesses! It can cry and scream all day, yet never become hoarse. What harmony it can sustain!

To know harmony is to know what is eternal. To know what is eternal is to be enlightened.

Do not try to add to your vitality; an energetic heart will exhaust you, and shorten your life. Once you are an adult, you are on the verge of old age and death. Excessive energy is not the Way; and that which is not the Way, soon dies.

Knowing and talking

Those who know, do not talk. Those who talk, do not know.

Close every window; shut every door; make every knife blunt; untangle every knot; dim every light. Do not allow yourself to be influenced or controlled by anyone or anything. Do not allow yourself to be influenced or controlled by calculations of profit or loss. Do not allow yourself to be influenced by praise or disgrace.

Let your wheels move only along old ruts. There is a sacred mystery in doing the same as people have always done. You will be honoured by heaven.

56

Political freedom

In ruling his country the king should do what is expected. In winning a war he should do what is unexpected. In controlling the world, a person should do nothing. How do I know this? By means of knowledge.

The more rules and regulations there are in the world, the poorer people become. The more experts a country has, issuing edicts on every aspect of life, the more confused people become.

The more skilful people are, the more ingenious their inventions, the more loudly they demand that the king provides policemen to protect their wealth. And as more policeman roam the land, so thieves and fraudsters become more adept.

Thus the wise leader says: 'I shall do nothing, and let the people look after themselves. I shall enjoy tranquillity, and let the people find justice for themselves. I shall avoid interfering in the conduct of business, and let the people prosper on their own. I myself am free from desire; let those who are wise among my people share my freedom.'

57

The small dark light

When the government is dull and inert, the people are contented and placid. When the government is eager and sharp, the people are discontented and devious.

Beneath happiness lies misery; happiness sits on a cushion of misery. Who knows when misery and happiness will end, and there will be peace? Nothing is certain.

That which people come to regard as normal, eventually reveals itself as monstrous. That which people regard as fortunate, eventually reveals itself as unfortunate. That which seems to educate people, eventually is shown to confuse them. There is no end to the perversity of the world.

And so wise people shape the wood of life without carving it; they make it square without sawing it; they make it smooth without sanding it. Wisdom is the light that does not shine – the small dark light.

The inactive ruler

In ruling the people and in serving heaven, it is best for a
ruler to be inactive. If he is inactive from the start of his rule,
the people will soon learn to expect inactivity from him; and
thus they will learn to rule themselves. As a result his country will enjoy an abundance of virtue; and he himself will be
invulnerable, because he will have no enemies.

When the inactive ruler decides on rare occasions to be
active, no one will oppose him, because they will have forgotten how to oppose. Thus the inactive ruler has unlimited
power. But he will retain this power only so long as he uses
it sparingly.

The inactive ruler is like a tree with deep roots and a
strong trunk. The less a ruler uses his power, the longer he
keeps it.

Lying low and riding high

Rule a large country in the manner you would cook a small fish.

If you exercise power in accordance with the Way, then people will not be violent or disruptive. This does not mean that people will be weak; it means they will not use their strength against you or one another.

If you exercise your power in accordance with the Way, wise people will flourish. People will not threaten them, but listen to them. In this way people will use their energy for the common good, and they will live together in harmony.

A good ruler is like the lower reaches of a river, where all the streams come together. A good ruler is like a tranquil woman. By remaining calm at all times, and not responding to her husband's foolish whims, she dominates him. In the same way the good ruler, by remaining calm in crises, and by not reacting to the foolish schemes that people may propose, dominates his country. The woman, lying quietly beneath the man, is mentally on top of him; the ruler, lying low, rides high.

60, 61

Honouring the Way

The home of every living being on earth is the Way. Good living beings know its value; weak living beings take refuge in it.

Rich people can pay others to be eloquent and to undertake acts of charity on their behalf. Wealth can purchase both fine words and fine deeds.

Imagine the coronation of the king. After the ceremony he appoints three men as his ministers; and they receive gifts brought by nobleman from throughout the country. What would you bring? A screen made of jade? It would be better to sit still, and let the Way be your offering.

Why was the Way honoured in days of old? People believed that, if they sought the Way, they would find it. And they believed that if they needed shelter, the Way would provide it. Thus the Way was honoured above all things under heaven.

Small and easy

Do without doing. Act without action. Taste without tasting any flavour. Treat the small as large, and the few as many.

When you are injured, respond with a kind deed. When you are insulted, respond with a kind word.

When life is easy, prepare for hard times. Solve problems that are small, before they grow large. Remember that even the greatest problems in the world were originally tiny problems.

Thus wise people, by never doing great things, get great things done.

It may be said that, if you only do small tasks, your work will be worthless. It may be said that, if you only do easy tasks, you show yourself to be feeble. But wise people know that by undertaking only small tasks, they achieve much; and that by only doing easy tasks, they show their strength.

Wanting not to want

It is easy to keep hold of that which has not stirred. It is easy to plan what has not occurred. It is easy to shatter that which is fragile. It is easy to scatter small things. It is easy to dissolve that which is tiny. It is easy to deal with a problem while it is still small.

A tree, which is so large your arms cannot reach round its trunk, grew from a seedling. The tower, which is nine storeys high, began with one brick being laid on another. A long journey starts with a single pace.

If you are constantly doing things, you will do wrong. If you are constantly acquiring possessions, you will lose some. Wise people do nothing, and so do no wrong. Wise people possess nothing, so they lose nothing.

Every undertaking goes wrong, just when people think it is complete.

Thus wise people want not to want; they strive not to strive; they learn not to be learned; they seek the place of not seeking; they work to achieve nothing – because they accept things as they are.

64

The virtue of ignorance

Long ago, when rulers ruled according to the Way, they did not try to make people clever, because they knew that clever people are difficult to rule. Instead they ensured that the people remained ignorant.

These rulers, who ruled according to the Way, did not try to be clever themselves; they knew that a ruler's clever schemes are a curse on the land. On the contrary, they ruled as if they were ignorant, knowing that a ruler's ignorance is a blessing on the land.

It is hard to understand why ignorance is a blessing; it requires wisdom to make ignorance your pattern and model. The virtue of ignorance is mysterious.

The mysterious virtue of ignorance is deep. It reaches far down into the mind, and stretches far back into the past. Deep in the mind, and at the beginning of time, there was unity.

The lower and the higher

The lake is master of the river that runs into it. Why? Because the lake is lower and the river is higher; and that which is lower, is master of that which is higher.

The wise person, wanting to teach other people, talks to them from below. The wise person, wanting to guide other people, follows them.

So the wise person advises without cajoling, leads without forcing, educates without informing. The wise person never competes for attention with others, knowing that competition is always futile.

As a result, people never tire of listening to the wise person's words, and praising the wise person's insight.

66

Three treasures

Everyone says that the Way is great, but resembles nothing they have known before. That which is truly great, cannot resemble anything else, because everything else is less great. That which resembles other things, cannot be truly great, but is trivial and dull.

I have three treasures that I hold and cherish. The first is compassion; the second is frugality; and the third is modesty. If you are compassionate, you will be prompted to be brave, in order to protect those for whom you feel compassion. If you are frugal, you can afford to be generous, because your wealth and abilities exceed your needs. If you are modest, with no desire to lead others, people will want you to lead them, knowing that you will not oppress or exploit them.

But to be brave without compassion, generous without frugality, or a leader without modesty, is disastrous.

Compassion wins the battle and holds the fort; it is the protection that heaven provides.

67

Victory through retreat

The fine general does not appear formidable. The brave warrior is never roused in anger. The successful fighter is reluctant to engage the enemy. The good leader shares the hardships of those beneath him.

If you wish to win, do not compete. If you wish to prove your prowess, do not boast. Simply follow heaven's lead.

The expert in warfare says: 'Rather than advance onto enemy ground, I'd prefer to let the enemy advance onto my ground. Rather than advance a small distance, I'd rather retreat a large distance.'

This is marching without marching, rolling up your sleeves without flexing your muscles, being armed without wielding weapons. It consists in giving the attacker no opponent. Nothing is worse that attacking what yields; nothing causes more frustration to those hostile to you, than to retreat in the face of their advance.

When two armies meet, the retreating army wins.

Sick of being sick

My words are easy to understand, and easy to follow. Yet nobody in the world fully understands them, or completely follows them.

True words have an ancestry that can be traced back to the earliest times. Right deeds, which come from following true words, require great mastery. Where this ancestry and this mastery are unknown, so am I.

Wise people wear their jade under their common clothes. Similarly my obscurity signifies my value.

To know, and yet to think that you do not know, is best. Not to know, and yet to think that you do know, is a sickness. The only cure for such sickness is to be sick of being sick.

Wise people are not sick. They are sick of being sick, so they are well.

70, 71

Knowledge and love

If you do not fear what should be feared, you are in great danger.

If you oppress others, and take pride in their subjugation, you are a fool; they will soon rise up against you, and trample you under their feet. If you exploit others, and take pleasure in the wealth you obtain from their work; they will soon rise up against you, and seize what is rightfully theirs.

Do not treat people as if they were stupid; then they will not act stupidly.

Wise people know themselves, but do not display their knowledge; they love themselves, but do not flaunt their love. Wise people are shrewd in choosing their friends, and shrewd in avoiding potential enemies.

72

Bravery and caution

The person who is both brave and daring, is likely to die young. The person who is both brave and cautious, is likely to live long. So be brave, but in each situation be cautious in deciding how to respond.

Heaven hates what it hates. Who can know the reason? Wise people do not even try to understand.

If you follow the Way, laid down by heaven, you will win without competing; you will answer questions without speaking; you will attract people without summoning them; you will perform difficult tasks without effort.

The net of heaven is cast wide, and its mesh is wide; yet it misses nothing.

73

Green and brown leaves

If the people had no fear of death, then their ruler could not subjugate them with threats of death. But since people fear death, the executioner enforces the ruler's will.

The rich tax the poor, causing the poor to starve. The people rebel, so the rich suppress them with violence. Thus the people come to hold life cheap, while the rich regard life as precious. In this way the poor gain wisdom, while the rich remain foolish; the poor learn that life should not be lived for the sake of living.

A living being is soft and tender; when it dies, it becomes hard and brittle. Look at the green leaves on the trees; then look again at the leaves after they have turned brown and fallen. So hardness and brittleness go with death, while softness and tenderness go with life. Men and women with hard hearts are dead, even while they remain alive; men and women with soft and tender hearts are alive, even after they have died.

74, 75, 76

A bow ready to shoot

The Way is like a bow that has been pulled, ready to shoot an arrow: its top end is brought down, and its lower end is raised up. The Way brings down the high and mighty, and raises up the lowly and humble. It takes from those who have much, and gives to those who have little.

The Way is not the normal human way. The normal human way is to take from those who have little, and give to those who have much. What can ensure that everyone has enough? Only the Way can ensure this.

Wise people accomplish much, but claim no credit; they teach much, but assert nothing; they are worth much, but desire no praise.

77

Right words sounding wrong

Nothing in this world is as soft and weak as water. Yet nothing is so effective as water at wearing away stones, which are hard and strong. And as it wears away stones, it remains unaltered. Thus softness overcomes hardness; weakness overcomes strength. Everyone knows this; but few people use this knowledge.

Wise people say: 'By regarding yourself as a sinner, you become virtuous. By regarding yourself as lowly, you become mighty.' Yes, life is full of paradoxes, in which right words sound wrong.

After a conflict is over, some enmity remains. How can peace be made? Wise people keep to the agreement that was made, but do not make demands on their former enemies.

Those whose power is genuine, concentrate on fulfilling their own obligations. Those whose power is hollow, insist on others fulfilling their obligations.

The Way has no favourites; it is on the side of goodness.

78, 79

A free people

Imagine a small country; and imagine that its people are free.

They have many tools, but rarely use them. They are aware of danger, and so avoid journeys abroad. They possess ships and carriages, and do not want to use them. They have armour and weapons, but never go to war. They possess implements with which to write, but have nothing to express.

They enjoy eating. They take pleasure in having colourful clothes. They have warm, comfortable houses, with which they are content. They observe the customs that they inherited from their ancestors.

The next country is so close that they can hear the cocks crowing and the dogs barking across the border. But they grow old and die without ever having been there.

80

Gain without loss

True words are not charming; and charming words are not true. Good people are not contentious; and contentious people are not good. People with real knowledge are not learned; and learned people lack real knowledge.

Wise people do not hoard wealth or possessions. The more people help others, the more they will receive help in times of need. The more people give to others, the more people will give to them in times of famine. Thus those who make themselves poor through generosity, are rich.

If you follow the Way, you will gain much without causing others to lose anything. You will succeed without causing others to fail. You will win without causing others to lose. The Way is the way of the wise.

81

CHUANG TZU

Chuang Tzu is the first Taoist teacher whose existence is beyond doubt; he lived in the fourth century BCE. The book bearing his name is an extraordinary collection of stories, jokes, witty aphorisms and philosophical discourses. Sometimes he appears as the central figure in a story; but many stories do not include him. Sometimes words are directly attributed to him; but many discourses have no attribution. So the book is an anthology, with little effort to harmonize the style of the pieces. The first seven chapters are generally regarded as the core, written either by him or by those who knew him personally, while the other chapters are probably the work of later disciples.

Small and great

One person goes out to his fields for the day; he leaves home in the morning, taking with him his lunch; and he returns home in the evening. A second person sets out on a journey to another town, knowing that he will be away from home for several days; he takes a bag of food on his back. A third person decided to visit another country, and will be away for several months; he takes a cart piled high with food.

The experience of these three people cannot be compared. A single day cannot be compared with several days; and several days cannot be compared with several months. How do we know this? The mushroom does not see the waxing and the waning of the moon. The butterfly does not see spring and autumn. There is a monster, living in the far south of the world, for whom five hundred years are like a season. There is a giant tree for whom eight thousand years are like a season.

There is a huge bird, whose name is Roc, and whose wings spread across the sky. He rises up on a whirlwind, soars through the clouds, and breaks through the blueness above. A quail laughs at him, saying: 'Where are you going? I leap up in the air, and come down again in the bushes a short distance away. That is the best way of flying.' The quail and Roc show the difference between that which is small and that which is great.

The king and the holy man

The loving person has no self. The wise person takes no credit. The holy person desires no praise.

Chuang Tzu once paid a visit to a king. After they had conversed for a while, the king said: 'When the sun rises, there is no point in keeping torches lit. When the rains come, there is no point in watering the ground. Now that you have come, there is no point in my continuing to rule. If you were to rule this country, there would be perfect order; but while I continue to rule, there is disorder.'

Chuang Tzu replied: 'Your rule is not perfect, but it is good. If I were to become ruler, people would think that I wanted fame and wealth for myself; and as a consequence of these thoughts there would not be perfect order. If I were to act as king, I should be like a guest who had taken over the home of his host.'

The king looked disappointed. Chuang Tzu concluded: 'The bird makes its nest deep in the forest, but uses only one branch. The animal drinks from the river, but takes only what it needs. The cook may not run the kitchen well, but the priest does not take his place.'

I

The cream for red hands

There was a family whose occupation was to bleach silk. Since they were constantly dipping their hands in the bleach, the skin on their hands became red and sore. Then a member of the family invented a cream that cured this soreness and protected the skin. The recipe for this cream was handed down from one generation to another for many centuries; and none of the family ever again suffered from red, sore hands.

Then one day a traveller, who happened to be passing by, noticed members of the family rubbing the cream onto their hands. 'What is the purpose of this cream?' he asked. And they explained the purpose to him. 'I should like to buy the recipe for this cream,' he said. So they took him to the head of the family; and the traveller paid a hundred gold coins. The head of the family was delighted, saying to the other members: 'For centuries we have earned no more than a few gold coins for our work. But now in a single day we get a hundred coins.'

The traveller then went to the king, who was about to send his army northwards, in order to suppress some rebels. The traveller said: 'In the cold northern winds the soldiers' hands will become red and sore, and they will not be able to wield their swords properly. As a result the rebels might defeat them. Let me go with the army, and cure this problem.' The king agreed. The traveller made a large quantity of the cream, and put it on a cart. Every morning he gave some cream to every soldier, and ordered him to rub it into his hands. As a result the army was victorious. And the king rewarded the traveller with a vast estate.

The useless tree

A man said to Chuang Tzu: 'I have a big tree that is utterly useless. Its trunk is so knotted that no carpenter can saw it; and its branches are so twisted that they cannot be turned into handles for tools. What shall I do?'

Chuang Tzu said: 'Look at the weasel. It is small and agile; it crouches in the undergrowth until it sees its prey – and then leaps out. But weasels rarely live long; they usually leap onto a trap, and are killed. Now look at the yak. It is big and clumsy, and can catch nothing. But yaks usually live to a great age. The fact that your tree is so useless is the reason why it will survive. Sit under its branches each day, and meditate on that.'

I

Mushrooms in damp earth

True wisdom is wide and tranquil; false wisdom is narrow and busy. Wise words are precise and clear; foolish words are petty and mean.

When you sleep, your spirit roams the earth as a peaceful observer. But when you wake, you become entangled with everything and everybody you encounter. Day by day your mind is caught up with problems – some trivial, some deep, and some intense. Minor troubles make you anxious; major troubles upset and disturb you. You are convinced you know right from wrong, and you struggle to impose the right solution to each problem. You cling to your views and prejudices, as if you had taken an oath of loyalty to them. Yet your solutions are like blocked drains; they cause the problems to stagnate.

Joy and anger, sadness and delight, hope and disappointment, doubt and belief, diligence and sloth, eagerness and reticence – all these are like mushrooms springing up from the damp earth. One will spring up, and last for a day, to be replaced by another. And no one knows where they sprout from.

Day and night exist. That is all we know for certain. Let us be content with that.

2

Clinging to life

You receive your bodily form at birth; and through your life you cling onto it, waiting for the end. Often you clash with other people; sometimes you impose your will on them, sometimes you submit to their will. You pass through the years like a galloping horse, and nothing can stop you.

Are you not pathetic? You toil and sweat till the end of your days, accomplishing many things, but enjoying none. You exhaust yourself to such a degree that you forget how to rest. Are you not a pitiful spectacle? 'I'm not dead yet!' you cry defiantly. But what good is there is staying alive? Your body gradually decays, and your mind soon follows. Can you deny your sorrow and suffering?

Human life has always been like this. Am I the only one to notice?

2

Circumstances and standards

If you allow your mind to guide you, then you will never be without a teacher. Why do you allow yourself to be taught by circumstances, which are constantly changing? Only fools are taught by circumstances. Why do you allow yourself to be taught by standards of right and wrong? All moral standards are inventions – and hence are arbitrary.

Words are not just hot air; words are used because they express things. Yet if a word cannot be defined, its meaning is uncertain. People suppose that words are different from the cheeps of birds. Yet is there really any difference? Words are used to specify standards of right and wrong. But the Way cannot be expressed in words, because it cannot be defined. The Way is known only within the mind.

2

Difference and completeness

Compare life with death, and compare death with life. Since there is life, there must be death; and since there is death, there must be life.

Compare the possible with the impossible, and compare the impossible with the possible. Since some things are possible, others are impossible; and since some are impossible, others are possible.

Compare the acceptable with the unacceptable, and compare the unacceptable with the acceptable. Since some forms of behaviour are acceptable, others are unacceptable; and since some forms of behaviour are unacceptable, others are acceptable.

Compare what is with what is not, and what is not with what is. Since some things are, other things are not; and since some things are not, other things are.

But the point at which there are no opposites, is the pivot of the Way; it is the centre of the circle. At this point the difference between opposites becomes their completeness; and their completeness becomes their difference.

2

The monkey trainer

Compare a little stalk with a great pillar, a leper with a beautiful woman, a comic event with a tragic event; the Way brings them all into unity. Through the Way their differences make them one. But only the wise person, with profound insight, understands this; the wise person never puts people or things into categories, but treats them all the same.

A monkey trainer was handing out acorns. He said to the monkeys: 'You will each get three in the morning and four in the evening.' This made the monkeys furious. So the trainer said: 'Very well, you will get four in the morning and three in the evening.' The monkeys were delighted. There was no difference between the monkey trainer's two statements; but one provoked anger, and the other joy. Wise people are like the monkey trainer; they present the truth in such a manner that it provokes joy.

Wise people are guided by the light that shines out of chaos; that is why they see things with clarity.

2

A single hair

I shall make a statement. I do not know whether my statement is compatible with what other people say; but one statement is much like another.

There is the beginning; there is a time when the beginning has not yet begun; there is a time when that time has not yet begun. There is being; there is a time when being has not yet come into being; there is a time when that time has not yet begun.

There is nothing in this world bigger than a single hair; the largest mountain is as small as a hair. No one lives longer than a dead child. Heaven and earth were born the same time as I was. All living beings are one with me.

Since all living beings are one, how can one living being say anything to another living being? Yet I have just said that all living beings are one. So how can I not be saying something?

The Way has no boundaries; words can mean what you want them to mean. But people make boundaries by inventing theories and by dividing things into categories. I say that those who make boundaries, fail to divide; wise people understand the unity of all that exists.

2

The nameless

The great Way is not named. Great disagreements should not be spoken. Great benevolence is not truly benevolent. Great modesty is not truly humble. Great courage is not violent.

If the Way is named and defined, it is not the Way. When speech is used to express disagreement, it is an abuse of words. If everyone were benevolent, no one would succeed in doing good to others. If modesty is fastidious and self-conscious, it should not be trusted. If courage takes pleasure in violence, it is pointless.

Understanding should be based on what it does not understand.

2

Knowing and not knowing

A disciple called Yeh asked Chuang Tzu: 'Do you know what everyone agrees upon?' 'How can I possibly know that?' Chuang Tzu said. 'Do you know what you do not know?' Yeh asked. 'How can I possibly know that?' Chuang Tzu said. 'Then does nothing know anything?' Yeh asked. 'How can I possibly know that?' Chuang Tzu said.

Chuang Tzu continued: 'Nevertheless I want to try and say something. How can I know what I claim to know? It might be what I do not know. Similarly, how can I not know what I think I do not know? It might be what I do know.'

2

Jumbled standards

Chuang Tzu said to his disciple Yeh: 'If a man sleeps in a damp place, he will awake to find his entire body aching and his limbs stiff. But is it the same for an eel? If a man climbs a tree, he will reach the top shaking and trembling with fear. But is it the same for a monkey? Is a man, an eel or a monkey most correct in choosing the right place to live?

'Humans eat meat of animals that feed on grass. Deer eat grass. Centipedes devour snakes. Crows enjoy mice. Which of these four is correct in choosing the right food to eat?

'A male monkey mates with a female monkey. A male fish enjoys the favours of a female fish. A man might say that a certain woman is very beautiful. But if he showed that woman to a male fish, the fish would dive to the bottom of the lake; if he showed her to a male bird, the bird would fly into the air; if he showed her to a deer, the deer would run away. Is the fish, the bird, the deer or the man correct in assessing beauty?

'Standards of good and bad, right and wrong, are jumbled up. No one can be certain of the difference between them.'

Yeh asked: 'In that case, do perfect people have no conception of right and wrong, good and bad?

Chuang Tzu replied: 'Perfect people do not feel the heat of burning deserts, nor the cold of deep oceans. They are not frightened by lightening that can split mountains, nor by storms that can whip up huge waves. They are indifferent to life and death. So they have no interest in standards of right and wrong, good and bad.'

Embracing the universe

Wise people do not labour at anything. They do not look for advantage or profit. They do not try to act benevolently towards other living beings, nor do they harm other living beings. They do not relish people treating them with respect and seeking their advice. They do not strive to follow the Way. They speak without speaking; and when they speak, they say nothing. They look beyond the confines of this dusty world.

How can wise people lean on the sun and the moon, and embrace the universe? They do this by seeing the oneness of all things; in the diversity of living beings, they see unity. Wise people have no concern for status; they do not see one living being as more worthy of honour than another. They are indifferent to power; they abhor the notion of one living being having control of another. They regard all living beings as equal. Most people strive to gain status and power, and look on wise people as naive and stupid.

2

Life as a dream

How do I know that love of life is not an illusion? How do I know that the fear of death is not like a young person running away from home, and then not being able to find the path back? There was once a beautiful young woman who lived in a land just beyond the border of China. The king's army captured that land, seized the young woman, and took her away. She wept so much at leaving her home and parents that she drenched all her clothes. Then she was taken to the king, who fell in love with her. Soon she was living in his palace, sharing his bed, and eating his food – and she wondered why she had ever felt sad. Perhaps the dead now wonder why they ever clung to life. How do I know?

You may dream of enjoying a drunken feast; and when you awake, you may weep and moan, realizing that the feast was only a dream. You may dream of weeping and moaning; but when you awake, you may joyfully go out hunting, realizing that your sadness was only a dream. When you dream, you do not know that you are dreaming; indeed, you may even dream of interpreting dreams. It is only when you awake, that you know you were dreaming. Eventually the day of judgement will dawn, when you will realize that all life is a dream. Only fools think that they are now awake and know what is really happening.

In life one person is the king and another person the servant; but those positions are no more than dreams.

2

Disagreements and uncertainties

Suppose you and I had an argument; and suppose you got the better of me. Does that prove that you are right and I am wrong? If I got the better of you, would that prove that I am right and you are wrong? Is it possible that both of us are wrong – or even that both of us are right? If you and I disagree on the matter at hand, then other people may be even less certain. So whom can we ask to judge between us? If we were to ask someone who agrees with you, or agrees with me, that would not be fair. If we were to ask someone who disagrees with both of us, then that person could not judge in favour of one of us – so our disagreement would remain unresolved. If we were to ask someone who agrees with both of us, then that person would be equally incapable of judging between us. So we must conclude that neither you nor I nor anyone else knows the answer for certain.

To wait for a single voice that will resolve all uncertainties and disagreements, is as pointless as waiting for nothing. Let all things be as they are, and change as they wish – and yet see the heavenly harmony in all things. What do I mean by heavenly harmony? I mean that right is wrong, and wrong is right. I mean that truth is false, and falsehood is true. If right were clearly right, then there would be no disagreement. If truth were clearly true, then there would be no uncertainty.

So stop worrying about the passing years. Stop making distinctions between right and wrong, truth and falsehood. Plunge into the unknown, and make it your home.

A man and a butterfly

A penumbra said to its shadow: 'You are in a perpetual state of flux. One moment you are walking, and the next you are standing still; one moment you are sitting, and the next you are standing up. Why can't you make up your mind?' The shadow replied: 'The body, of which I am a shadow, determines what I do. But I wonder whether this body is controlled by some other body. How can I know?'

A man once dreamt he was a butterfly. In his dream he flitted from one flower to another, enjoying himself. Then he awoke, and saw that he was a man. But then he reflected on the process of dreaming and waking — and became confused. He wondered if he had dreamt of waking from the dream in which he was a butterfly. He asked himself: 'Am I a man who has dreamt he was a butterfly? Or am I a butterfly who is dreaming he is a man?' So all of us should wonder if there is any distinction between a human and a butterfly.

2

Avoiding rewards and punishments

Your life has a limit, but knowledge has none. To use that
which is limited, in order to pursue that which has no limit,
is dangerous. If you understand this, and yet still strive for
knowledge, you will certainly run into trouble.

If you sincerely wish to do good, then avoid rewards. If
you wish to do evil, then avoid punishments.

Follow the middle course, because by this means you will
stay in one piece. Keep yourself alive, and look after your parents, and enjoy the years left to you.

3

Cutting meat

A cook was butchering an ox for his master. Every movement of his hand, every heave of his shoulder, every step of his feet, and every thrust of his knee, was in perfect accord with his task, enabling him to cut the meat with supreme efficiency. He was as elegant as a dancer.

His master was watching him, and exclaimed: 'This is wonderful. How has your skill reached such heights?' The cook put down his knife, and said: 'My greatest love is the Way, which is finer than any skill. When I first began butchering animals, I could only see the animal itself. Now I am no longer guided by my eyes; instead I am guided by what my mind understands and perceives. Thus I perceive the natural lines of the animal, and my knife follows those lines. I perceive the weak points in the animal's flesh, and my knife pierces those points. I never touch the smallest ligament or tendon, let alone any bone. An ordinary cook has to change his knife every month, because he hacks at the meat. But I have been using this knife for nineteen years, and its blade is as sharp as when I first obtained it.'

'What do you do when you come to a difficult part of the animal?' the master asked. The cook replied: 'I consider carefully what to do, and move with great caution. Very gently I move the knife until the flesh falls apart easily.'

The master said: 'I have watched and listened to my cook, and have learned how to live fully.'

3

A teacher's death

When a particular spiritual teacher died, Chuang Tzu came to his funeral. When Chuang Tzu arrived, he gave three loud shouts – and then left.

One of the disciples of the dead teacher ran after Chuang Tzu, and remonstrated with him. Chuang Tzu said: 'I was astonished to find all his disciples weeping and wailing, and giving speeches in his honour. Yet he never taught his disciples to weep and wail, and he never asked them to honour him. On the contrary, he taught his disciples to accept all things as they are. He was born when he was due to be born, and he died when he was due to die; so there is no cause for sadness.'

3

Fame and knowledge

Do you know how virtue is ruined, or where knowledge comes from? Virtue is ruined by fame, and knowledge comes from debate. In their struggle for fame people destroy one another; and they use knowledge as a means for doing this. Thus you should have nothing to do with either fame or knowledge.

You may have great virtue, and your sincerity may be beyond question; you may be kind-hearted and humble. But if you do not understand how people feel and think, you will not do good, but you will do great harm.

You may be so keen for people to be benevolent that you try to compel them to act benevolently. Your motive may be entirely pure. But people will hate you for what you are doing.

Keep your advice to yourself. If people think they are already virtuous, they will resent your telling them how to be more virtuous. If people prefer vice to virtue, they will not listen to you.

Listening with the soul

Do not listen with your ears, but listen with your mind. No, do not listen with your mind, but listen with your soul. The ears only hear sounds; the mind only recognizes sounds; but the soul understands sounds.

It is easy to stop walking; but it is difficult to walk without your feet touching the ground. It is easy to be hypocritical, giving the impression to others that you are different from your true self; but it is difficult to maintain your hypocrisy in relation to heaven. It is easy to fly with wings; but it is difficult to fly without wings. It is easy to know by means of knowledge; but it is difficult to know by means of having no knowledge.

If you cannot keep your body still, you will not be able to keep your mind still. A restless body leads to a restless mind, that races off in all directions.

Use your ears and eyes to hear and see what is within yourself. Use your soul and mind to feel and know what is outside yourself.

4

Destiny and duty

In everything you do, whether great or small, success only comes if you follow the Way. Yet if you desire success, you will suffer, because yin and yang will be disturbed. To avoid this suffering, you must be indifferent to success and failure.

In this world there are two great principles: one is destiny, and the other is duty. The love of a child for its parents is a matter of destiny; that love is written on the child's soul. The obedience of subjects to their ruler is a matter of duty; that obedience is given in order to avoid punishment and preserve peace. To accept your destiny with neither resentment nor elation — that is a matter of duty.

4

Human relationships

Let me teach you some important lessons about human relationships.

If two people are living close to one another, they may form a bond through personal contact. But if two people live far apart, they have to rely on messages conveyed through others. But trying to convey emotions and feelings through messages is the hardest task under heaven. Messages tend to exaggerate people's true feelings: if they are happy with one another, messages are laden with excessive praise; if they feel a little irritated, their messages seem burdened with violent anger. So if you are conveying messages to another person, make light of your feelings.

When people gather to pit their strength and agility against one another in sport, they begin in a friendly mood; but the mood inevitably changes to aggression. As the tension mounts, they resort to tricks and deceit in order to win. Similarly when men come together to drink at some festival, their behaviour is initially retrained and courteous; but it gradually degenerates into rowdiness. The same is true of all human gatherings; they begin well, and end badly.

Words are like wind over the sea. At first there is a gentle breeze, and all is calm; then a gale blows up, and soon there are waves of rage and anger. But do not allow yourself to be stirred. Observe what occurs, but remain firmly on the Way.

4

Insects, tigers and horses

Do you know about the praying mantis, that waved its arms angrily in front of an approaching carriage? It had such a high opinion of its own abilities, that it thought it could bring the carriage to a halt. Be careful; be on your guard. If you put too much confidence in your own talents, you will be in grave danger.

Do you know how the tiger trainer protects himself. He does not give them living animals to eat, in case this engenders in them a love of killing. Nor does he give them whole carcasses, in case the act of tearing these apart excites them too much. He gauges their appetite and understands their ferocious disposition. Tigers are quite different from humans; yet the trainer can train them to be gentle, so long as he adapts his behaviour according to their nature. The trainer who went against the tigers' nature, would not last long.

People who love horses, collect their manure in baskets and their urine in bottles. Yet if a mosquito or gadfly lands on a horse, and the groom swipes it away, the horse may break its bit, damage its harness, and hurt its chest. Out of affection the groom tries to do good, but in fact does harm. So in all you do you should exercise great caution.

4

The worthless oak tree

A carpenter and his apprentice were passing through a village, where on the village green stood a huge oak tree. It was the largest tree the apprentice had ever seen, and he stared at it in wonder for several minutes; the carpenter did not even glance up, but continued walking.

The apprentice had to run to catch up with the carpenter. 'Were you not impressed with that vast oak tree?' the apprentice asked. The carpenter replied: 'It's so old and knotted as to be worthless. Make boats out of it, and they'd sink. Make coffins out of, and they'd rot. Make doors out of it, and they would sweat sap. Make posts out of it, and the worms would eat them.'

That night the carpenter had a dream, in which the oak tree appeared to him and spoke: 'Are you comparing me with fruit trees, such as cherry, apple and plum? At the end of the summer people come along and steal their fruit − pulling their branches in all directions as they do so. Are you comparing me with the great trees of the forest? Before they are fully grown people come and chop them down, and saw them into planks. I have strived hard to be worthless, because this protects me. Nobody pulls my branches and steals from me; and nobody has chopped me down.'

The following morning the carpenter said to his apprentice: 'That huge oak tree is a holy tree. Yesterday I judged it by conventional standards. But now I understand it − and I shall always treat it with reverence.'

4

The use of the useless

Shu is severely disabled. His back is so hunched that his head is lower than his shoulders and his pigtail is pointing to the sky. Through washing and mending other people's clothes, he earns enough to survive. When the king requires all able-bodied men to join his army, in order to fight some distant war, Shu stands in the crowd, waving them farewell. When a work party is required to perform some difficult and dangerous task, Shu is ignored. And when at festival times food is given away to the needy, Shu always receives an ample portion. So Shu's disability ensures his survival – while many able-bodied men are killed in the flower of youth.

Yu is mad. And in his madness he frequently cries out these wise words: 'You cannot wait for the future, and you cannot pursue the past. When the world follows the Way, wisdom succeeds; when the world abandons the Way, wisdom still survives. Good fortune is as light as a feather, but no one knows how to pick it up. Misfortune is heavier than earth, but no one knows how to avoid it. Give up trying to teach people virtue. Get out of my path. I may walk in a crooked fashion, but you must not impede me. The tall, straight trees on the mountain bring about their own destruction, because they make such excellent timber. Pure fat invites itself to be used in cooking. The lacquer tree seems to be begging to be hacked and cut. Everyone knows the use of that which is useful. But does anyone know the use of the useless?'

4

Still water

A man called Wang had his feet cut off as punishment for some offence. Subsequently many people came to regard him as a great spiritual teacher. He never gave lectures, nor did he offer advice. But people flocked to his house, and always came away satisfied. So in what did his greatness lie?

He was indifferent to both life and death. If heaven were to fall to the earth, and the earth were to collapse under its weight, he would not have been disturbed. He distinguished that which is eternal from that which is temporal; and he knew that within all temporal things lies an eternal element. His eyes and ears did not make judgements; they did not approve of one thing, and disapprove of another. Rather his eyes and ears discerned the inner harmony of all things – for he knew that the eternal element in all things is one. His mind did not weigh up gains and losses; he did not regard one event as a gain, and another as a loss. Rather his mind accepted all events with equanimity. Thus when his feet were cut off, he remarked with a smile: 'Two lumps of earth have been taken from the bottom of my legs.'

When people wish to see a reflection of themselves, they do not look in running water; they look in still water. Wang is inwardly still; so people see in him their true selves.

5

Ugly and attractive

There was a man called Ai, who was extremely ugly. Yet despite his ugliness, men were inspired by him. When he was with a group of men, all eyes would be turned towards him; and no one would ever leave the group until he did. And women found him attractive. Young women frequently said to their parents: 'I should rather be Ai's mistress than any other man's wife.'

Ai never took the lead in anything, but simply agreed with what others said. He held no position of power, so he was not able to enrich people or even feed them. So why did people flock to him?

The king himself was intrigued by that question; so he summoned Ai to his palace. When Ai arrived, the king was horrified by his ugliness; he was the ugliest man the king had ever seen. Nonetheless he invited Ai to stay. After about a month the king began to appreciate Ai's qualities; and after a year he had complete trust in him. So he invited Ai to become his chief minister. Ai gave an evasive answer, neither accepting nor refusing the king's offer. The king was embarrassed; but after a little hesitation, the king announced that Ai was now chief minister. That night Ai left the palace and returned home. The king was devastated, saying: 'I can no longer take pleasure in my power, because Ai will not share it with me.'

5

Piglets and a dead mother

I once saw a litter of piglets trying to suckle from their mother, who had just died. After a while the piglets ran away from her, because they realized that she was not the same as she had been. The piglets had loved their mother. But it was not her body that they loved; they loved that which gave her body life.

A soldier may win many medals for his valour; but when he is killed in battle, those medals become useless. A man may take pleasure in wearing fine shoes; but if his feet are amputated, shoes no longer hold any interest for him.

The consorts of the king do not cut their own nails, nor do they pierce their own ears. A courtier who has just married, is released from his duties in the palace for a time, so he can devote himself to his new wife.

Since so much care is devoted to the body, how much more care should be devoted to the cultivation of virtue!

5

Still water

What is perfect balance? Birth and death; preservation and loss; failure and success; poverty and wealth; honour and dishonour; praise and blame; hunger and thirst; cold and heat – all these come and go according to destiny. Day and night follow each other, and there is no means of knowing their source. But do not allow destiny to disturb your inner harmony; do not allow it to upset your mind. If you can take equal delight in all that destiny brings – and if you can do this day after day without break – then you have perfect balance.

Perfect balance is found in still water; and still water should be an example to us all. It has no shape and no colour; it is unaffected by anything outside itself; and it protects its own depths.

5

Bodies and characters

A man with no teeth and a man with a hunched back were close friends, spending much of their time in each other's company. When the toothless man saw people with straight backs, he thought their backs were abnormal and ugly. And when the hunchback saw people with mouths full of teeth, he thought their faces were abnormal and ugly.

A very short man and a very tall man were close friends, spending much of their time in each other's company. When the short man saw other short people, he thought their shortness was abnormal and ugly. When the tall man saw other tall people, he thought their tallness abnormal and ugly.

A very fat man and a very thin man were close friends, spending much of their time in each other's company. When the fat man saw other fat people, he thought their fatness was abnormal and ugly. When the thin man saw other thin people, he thought their thinness abnormal and ugly.

You should ignore bodies, and look only at characters. When people do not ignore what they should ignore, and ignore what they should not ignore, they are truly ignorant.

5

Glue and bandages

Wise people regard knowledge as a curse, social convention as a glue, benevolence as a bandage, and selling as begging. Wise people do not have ambitions or make schemes, so knowledge is useless to them. They do not make divisions, so glue is useless to them. They cause no harm to others, so bandages are useless. They want nothing, so begging is useless.

Wise people look like ordinary human beings, but they do not have ordinary emotions and feelings. Since they look like human beings, ordinary human beings seek out their friendship. But since they do not have ordinary emotions, the ordinary standards of right and wrong are irrelevant to them.

Wise people have bodies that are puny and small, like those of ordinary human beings; so they live on earth. Wise people have minds that are strong and broad; so they are at one with heaven.

When I say that wise people do not have ordinary feelings and emotions, I mean that they do not have likes and dislikes; so they are content to allow life to follow its own course.

Ordinary people wear themselves out with useless toil and pointless argument.

True people

Who are true people?

True people do not fight against poverty, nor do they seek fulfilment through riches; they do not plan their affairs. True people do not regret their failures, nor do they take pride in their successes. True people can scale great heights without fear; and they can go through fire without pain. True people have no difficulty in following the Way.

True people breathe from deep within themselves, whereas ordinary people breathe with their chests. True people neither love life nor hate death; they take no delight in life's pleasures, and they depart from life without fuss. They attach no importance to their origins, and they are not concerned about what will happen to them after death.

True people are both chilly like the early winter, and mild like the early summer. They accept all things as they are, and try to change nothing. They are generous to all people, but have no special favourites. They do not seek to impose their views on others, and they do not display their feelings.

True people do not crumble under pressure. They require little, and never regret what they lack. They can show annoyance when this is appropriate; but usually they are mild and tolerant. They like all people, but are attached to no one.

6

The boat and the net

Birth and death are fixed. They are as certain as the dawn that comes after the night. They are beyond the control of human beings. They are truths that must be accepted. People are often devoted to their ruler, and are willing to die for him. How much more willing they should be to die for the sake of truth!

When the lakes dry up at the end of a hot summer, the fish are left stranded on the ground. They try to look after each other, wetting one another with their own slime. But it would be better if the lakes were full again, and the fish could ignore one another.

Birth imposes on each of us the burden of a physical form, and makes life a struggle. We each long for peace and rest in life; and we can look forward to peace in death. That which makes life good, also makes death good.

A fisherman hides his boat in a gorge and his fishing net in a pool, thinking they will be safe. But in the middle of the night a strong man comes and carries them off. Small-minded people imagine that hiding smaller things in bigger things will protect them. But if you were to hide the world in the world, so there was no space left, then nothing could be taken away.

Wise people encompass the whole world in their wisdom; so nothing can be taken from them.

6

Not high and not deep

The Way has reality, and it can be expressed; but it does nothing, and has no form.

The Way can be passed on, but it cannot be received. It can be obtained, but it cannot be seen.

The Way is rooted in itself. It has existed since before heaven and earth were born. It exists for all eternity. Indeed, the Way brought heaven and earth to birth.

The Way is above the atmosphere, but it cannot be called high. It is below the ocean, but it cannot be called deep. It is more ancient than antiquity, but it cannot be called ancient.

The Way brought the sun and the moon into existence; and since that moment they have never rested.

6

Learning the Way

There was a man called Yi. He was highly intelligent, but did not know the Way. I am not intelligent, but I know the Way. I wanted to teach him the Way; and I thought that teaching the Way to a man of intelligence would be easy.

I taught him for three days, and he was able to ignore worldly matters. I taught him for a further seven days, and he was able to ignore all external matters. I taught him for a further nine days, and he was able to ignore his own existence. He could now see with clarity. He realized that all things are one. The distinction between past and present, and between birth and death, now seemed irrelevant to him; he knew that the end of life is not death, and the coming to birth is not life. The distinction between giving and receiving, and between creating and destroying, now seemed irrelevant to him; he knew that in stillness there is movement, and that in movement there is stillness.

6

Becoming deformed

Two spiritual teachers, called Yu and Su, met. Yu said to Su:
'I look upon my head as nothing, my back as life, and my
bottom as death.' Su said to Yu: 'I regard life and death,
existence and annihilation, as one.' With this exchange they
became friends.

   Shortly afterwards Yu fell ill, becoming severely deformed.
Su went to visit him. Yu said: 'Look at me! My back is so
bent that my belly is above my chin, and my shoulders are
above my head. My yin and yang are in total disarray. Yet my
soul is calm and unworried.' With these words he limped to
a pool, looked at his own reflection, and smiled.

   'Do you dislike how you look?' Su asked. Yu replied: 'Not
at all. Perhaps my left arm will become like a cockerel, and I
shall know when dawn breaks. Perhaps my right arm will become a crossbow, and I shall be able to hunt. Perhaps my
bottom will become a carriage, and I shall be able to go for
a ride. I shall remain alive so long as I am meant to remain
alive, and I shall die when I am meant to die. I float happily
with the flow of nature, with no fears or anxieties. So why
should I dislike my appearance?'

6

The parents of humanity

A short time later Su fell fatally ill. As he lay on his bed, gasping and heaving, his wife and children were kneeling beside the bed, weeping and wailing. Yu came to visit, and said to Su's wife and children: 'Get out. You must not interrupt this process of change.' Su's wife and children left the room.

Then Su said: 'When parents tell their child to do something, the child obeys. Yin and yang are the mother and father of humanity. They have brought me close to death, and it would be perverse to try and disobey them. To them my death is not a cause for concern. During my life I have sought peace and tranquillity; now my death will be peaceful and tranquil. I look upon death just as I have looked upon life. A blacksmith would not be pleased if a piece of metal leapt up, and demanded to be made into a sword. Equally I have no right to leap up, and say to yin and yang that I demand to be turned into a healthy young man. I accept death as I accepted life.'

6

Response to death

An old woman died; and her son Meng did not weep. He mourned for her, but showed no signs of sadness or distress. Some people were critical, thinking that Meng could not have loved his mother. They expressed their view to Chuang Tzu.

Chuang Tzu replied: 'Meng is a person of deep understanding; he knows what he does not know. He knows that he does not know the mystery of birth and death. And in knowing what he does not know, he is content. He allows life to unfold, without trying to understand or control it.'

The people were baffled. So he continued: 'We are all in a constant process of change. Yet we cannot predict the results of this process, nor can we understand how it occurs. Perhaps you and I are in a dream, from which we shall eventually awake. When you recognize the constancy of change, you seek to protect your soul from it – and that is what Meng has done. His mother has changed from life to death; but his emotions are unchanged. Thus he is content, and nothing can wipe the smile from his mind.'

Then Chuang Tzu concluded: 'You dream you're a bird, soaring up into the air. You dream you're a fish, diving deep into a pool. But when you tell me about it, I do not know whether you were awake or dreaming. Passing judgement on others is not as good as laughing; and laughing is not as good as accepting things as they are. Accept Meng as he is, just as he accepts his mother's death.'

6

Ignoring everything

A man called Wen went to Chuang Tzu, and said: 'I have im-proved.' Chuang Tzu asked: 'How have you improved?' Wen replied: 'I now ignore conventional standards of morality.' Chuang Tzu said: 'That is good, but it is not enough.'

Some time later Wen returned to Chuang Tzu, and said: 'I have improved.' Chuang Tzu asked: 'How have you im-proved?' Wen replied: 'I now ignore religion and its rituals.' Chuang Tzu said: 'That is good, but it is not enough.'

Some time later Wen returned again, and said: 'I have im-proved.' Chuang Tzu asked: 'How have you improved?' Wen replied: 'I now ignore everything.' Chuang Tzu asked: 'What do you mean by that?' Wen replied: 'I could smash my limbs into pieces, and not be perturbed. I could go blind and deaf, and not be perturbed. I could lose my ability to think and speak, and not be perturbed. That is what I mean by ignor-ing everything.'

Chuang Tzu said: 'That is enough. You have learnt the Way.'

Looking for someone to blame

Yu and Sang were friends. Once it rained incessantly for ten days. Yu said to himself: 'This rain will have made Sang depressed, and he will not have eaten properly.' So Yu wrapped up some rice, and took it to his friend.

When he reached Sang's gate, he heard the sound of a lute, and the voice of someone singing: 'Oh, father! Oh, mother! Oh, heaven! Oh, humanity!' The voice sounded croaky, as if it were about to disappear; and the singer was rushing, as if he were anxious to complete his song.

Yu went inside, and asked: 'Why are you singing like this?' Sang replied: 'I was trying to work out what had made me depressed; but I couldn't find an answer. My father and mother surely would not wish me to be so melancholy. Heaven would not wish me to be so melancholy. I want to discover who is to blame – but I can't. So I suppose it must be destiny.' With that thought he became cheerful.

6

The bird and the mouse

It is often said that a ruler should establish the principles by which he intends to govern, should set the standards of behaviour which he expects of people, should devise ceremonies for people to observe, and should compose laws to regulate every aspect of people's lives.

But this will destroy people's natural virtue. To govern the world in this manner is like trying to walk on the ocean, drill a hole through a river, or make a mosquito carry a mountain.

When wise people govern, they do not concern themselves with external matters. They allow people to act in whatever ways are natural to them. The bird flies high in the sky to avoid being shot with arrows. The mouse burrows under the ground to avoid being hunted. We do not try to regulate how birds and mice behave. So why should we regulate how human beings behave?

7

Ruling the world

A man called Ken was wandering on the sunny side of the Yin mountain. He met Chuang Tzu, and said: 'I wish to ask you how the world should be ruled.'

Chuang Tzu replied: 'Get away from me, you stupid lout! What a dreary question you ask! I am following the Way. If that proves too tiring, I shall ride the bird of comfort, and go beyond the world; I shall wander in the land of nowhere, which is in the region of nothing. So why are you disturbing and upsetting me with questions about how to rule the world?'

Despite this answer Ken repeated his question. Chuang Tzu replied: 'Let your mind journey in simplicity. Be at one with that which is beyond definition. Let things be as they are. Have no personal views or opinions. That is how the world should be ruled.'

7

The enlightened ruler

A man called Yan went to see Chuang Tzu, and said: 'In my view a good ruler should be as swift as an echo, and as strong as a tree. He should be highly intelligent, with clarity of vision.'

Chuang Tzu replied: 'A ruler like that would merely exhaust his body and distress his mind. The tiger and the leopard are hunted because of the beauty of their hides. The dog and the monkey are kept in chains because of their agility. The strong and intelligent ruler is like these animals. The truly enlightened ruler would be quite different.'

'How would he be different?' Yan asked. Chuang Tzu replied: 'Do you really want to know about the enlightened ruler? His achievements would cover the world, yet he would do nothing. His authority would transform the world, yet no one would depend on him or obey him. He would neither promote one person above another, nor praise one person above another; he would let all people fulfil their own natures. His laws would be beyond definition, and he would reside in no particular place.'

7

The confused shaman

There was a shaman called Chi who could predict when people would die, and whether they would enjoy good or bad
fortune. Many people were frightened of him. But one person, called Zu, went to visit Chi, and was enthralled by him.

Zu then spoke to Chuang Tzu: 'You teach about the Way,
which is very fine. But I have found someone even wiser than
you – the shaman called Chi.' Chuang Tzu said: 'Bring this
shaman to me, that he and I may see each other.'

Zu brought Chi to see Chuang Tzu. After the meeting the
shaman said to Zu: 'I am very anxious about Chuang Tzu –
he is dying, and will be dead within a few days.' Zu was
very upset, and reported this prediction to Chuang Tzu.
Chuang Tzu smiled, and asked Zu to bring the shaman back
in a few days.

So a few days later Zu brought the shaman back to see
Chuang Tzu. After the meeting the shaman said: 'Chuang Tzu
is now better; he overflows with life.' Zu was very pleased,
and reported the shaman's words to Chuang Tzu. Chuang Tzu
smiled, and asked Zu to bring the shaman back in a few days.

So a few days later Zu brought the shaman back to see
Chuang Tzu. After the meeting the shaman said: 'Chuang Tzu
is never the same; I cannot discern his present state.' Zu reported these words to Chuang Tzu, and Chuang Tzu replied:
'I simply show myself to the shaman as I want him to see
me, and not as I am.' After this Zu forgot about the shaman,
and decided to study the Way.

Like a mirror

Do not hanker for fame. Do not make plans and devise schemes. Do not try to achieve anything. Do not try to acquire knowledge. Enjoy what you possess, but do not hold onto anything. Do whatever work you are capable of doing, but do not take pride in any task. Be empty.

The soul of a perfect person is like a mirror. A mirror does not search for things, nor does it seek to know anything; it simply responds. As a result of being like a mirror, the wise person can cope with anything, and is harmed by nothing.

7

Ducks and cranes

People skilled in debate construct arguments in the same way that bricklayers construct walls; they weave arguments in the same way that netmakers weave string. But whereas a net or a wall may be useful, an argument has no value. Arguments take people on the wrong path.

On the true path, which is the Way, people do not lose their inherent natures. They do not regard differences between themselves and others as causes of division. They accept themselves and others as they are.

The legs of a duck are short, and trying to lengthen them would cause pain; the legs of a crane are long, and trying to shorten them would cause pain. That which is naturally long, should not be cut; and that which is naturally short, should not be stretched. Defying nature solves nothing.

Is righteousness an inherent part of human nature? Look how much anxiety is caused by those who strive to be righteous. If your toes were webbed, separating them would cause great pain. If you had six fingers, cutting off the extra finger would cause great pain. Only be righteous if you are naturally righteous.

8

Making no changes

Do not apply a template to that which is naturally straight, in order to make it curved; and do not apply a plumb-line to that which is naturally curved, in order to make it straight. If something is square, do not use a compass to make it round; and if something is round, do not use a set square to make is square. If two things are separate, do not apply glue to stick them together; if something is dull, do not apply varnish to make it shiny. You should allow everything under heaven to remain in its natural form. And you should not try to understand why things are as they are; if you understand things, you will be more tempted to try and change them. A minor change to an object is liable to alter its purpose, while a major change is liable to alter its very nature.

Equally you should not try to change other people. Righteous men and women devote themselves to making others conform to their standards – and thereby do great damage. Greedy people devote themselves to exploiting others for their own advantage – and thereby do great damage. Scholars devote themselves to making other people respect them – and thereby do great damage. Rulers devote themselves to making others obey them – and thereby do great damage.

8

Good seeing and hearing

A father sent his son and daughter to tend his sheep, which were grazing on a hillside; but they lost the sheep. When the father asked the boy what happened, the boy replied that he was reading – and so did not notice the sheep disappearing. When the father asked the girl what happened, the girl replied that she was playing a game – and so did not notice the sheep disappearing. They were each doing something different, but they both lost the sheep. There are many different ways of being foolish, but only one way to be wise.

Wisdom has nothing to do with benevolence and righteousness; wisdom consists in being led by your own inherent nature – nothing more. When I urge you to have good hearing, I do not mean being able to hear external sounds clearly; I mean being able to hear yourself. When I urge you to have good eyesight, I do not mean being able to see external objects clearly; I mean being able to see yourself. People who only hear and see others, and never hear and see themselves, constantly try to control others, and they are constantly jealous of what others possess and enjoy.

Don't try to elevate yourself through acts of benevolence and righteousness; and do not sink into idiocy and folly.

8

The nature of horses

Horses have hooves so that their feet can grip on frost and snow, and hair so that they can withstand cold and wind. It is their nature to eat grass and drink water, to canter and to gallop. Even if grand castles and luxurious palaces were built for them, they would not be interested in them.

A man called Po went to see the king, and said: 'I am an expert in training horses.' The king entrusted ten of his finest young horses to Po, and ordered him to train them. Po branded them with a hot iron; he cut their hair and trimmed their hooves; he put halters over their heads and bridled them; and kept them in stalls within dingy stables. Three horses died. Then he deliberately gave them too little to eat and drink in order to make them lean; he raced them, using whips to make them gallop faster; and he covered them in all kinds of finery, and paraded them. Another three horses died. So as a result of Po's training only four out of the ten horses survived.

Many people in positions of power and influence in the world have the same attitude to other people as Po had towards horses.

9

The nature of humans

Human beings weave cloth to wrap around their bodies, and they till the soil to produce food for themselves; weaving and tilling are natural activities for humans. Human beings have strong, agile legs, which enable them to walk over any kind of terrain, and to cover large distances – so long as they walk slowly and carefully. Thus they have no need to build smooth roads, or to dig tunnels through the mountains. They like to keep sheep and cattle, and they understand how these animals like to live; so their flocks and herds multiply.

Human beings naturally regard one another as equals, and so they dislike hierarchies. They are happy to live simply, and so they have no innate desire to acquire great wealth. They are naturally generous and kind to one another, so they have no need for elaborate laws and moral codes to govern their behaviour. They have a natural sense of the oneness of all that exists, so religious ceremonies are useless to them – and besides, they naturally dislike fussing over rituals. The assertion of power by one person over others, and the imposition of religion and morality, are unnatural to human beings, and bring about great distress and misery.

9

Wisdom as folly

To guard yourself against thieves who slash open suitcases, rifle through bags, and smash open boxes, you should use straps and locks. This is what most people regard as wisdom. Yet if a thief is strong and cunning enough, he waits for the opportunity to carry away your box, your suitcase or your bag — and his only fear is that the strap and lock will break as he does so. Thus what seems like wisdom, turns out to be folly, because it helps the thief.

Wisdom in the eyes of the world is usually a sophisticated form of folly, helping people to perform evil deeds.

Long ago the state of Chi was famous for its good order, with a ruler famous for his wisdom. This ruler created an elaborate code of laws that ensured people behaved virtuously; and he built many temples, compelling people to worship in them. Then one morning a wicked man called Cheng killed the ruler, and took over the country. He did not change the laws or destroy the temples; on the contrary he upheld the laws and the religion that the good ruler had established. So order was maintained; and this enabled Cheng to plunder the people's wealth, and build himself vast palaces, with impunity. And Cheng's descendents retained power for twelve generations. Thus the apparent wisdom of the first ruler opened the gate for a long period of cruelty and oppression.

Learning to be natural

One person steals a small jade or pearl ornament, and he is executed; another person steals a country, and he becomes its ruler. Yet rulers never tire of passing laws and urging people to act righteously. So the lesson appears to be this: cultivate intelligence, so that your robberies may be large and bold.

If intelligence were destroyed, there would no longer be any great robberies. If every piece of jade and every pearl were shattered, petty thieving would cease. Equally if accounts and contracts were ripped up, people would live simple, happy lives. If weights and measures were cast away, people would no longer argue. If every law was rescinded, people would work out between themselves how to co-operate for their mutual advantage. If no one wore any kind of adornment, people would appreciate the natural beauty of the human form. If the template and the plumb-line, the compass and the set square, were abolished, people would use each material according to its nature.

The greatest skill in the world is to be natural.

10

Travelling to another country

In the distant past people lived naturally and simply. They enjoyed their food; they took pleasure in their clothes; they were content with their way of life; and they felt safe and comfortable in their own homes. People were healthy until their span of life was complete; then they died without pain. And they never travelled beyond their own borders. At that time perfect harmony was the norm.

Now people are agitated. They constantly imagine that there is a better way of life than the one they are currently leading. So they seek out wise men for advice. And they pack up their possessions, leave their parental homes, and go to other countries, in search of greater wealth, knowledge and excitement. You can see countless footprints and the tracks of the numerous carriages, marking these journeys between one country and another.

Do people ever attain greater happiness as a consequence of travelling from their native land? No, they become confused and miserable.

The distress of knowledge

The acquisition of knowledge does not bring any benefits. How do I know this?

It takes a great deal of knowledge to make longbows, crossbows, arrows, nets, and so on; but the result is that birds fly higher, in order to avoid being killed. It takes a great deal of knowledge to make fishing lines, traps, baits and hooks; but the result is that fish swim deeper. It takes a great deal of knowledge to make traps, snares and nets; but the result is that animals seek refuge in marshy lands where they cannot be caught.

In the same way it takes great mental agility to speak eloquently, to devise plots and schemes, to spread rumours, and to concoct clever arguments. But the result is that people are confused.

So the pursuit of knowledge causes great and needless distress to all that lives.

All human beings know how to seek knowledge that they do not possess; but few people know how to be satisfied with what they do not know. All human beings know how to condemn what they do not like; but few people know how to pass adverse judgement on themselves.

It is as if the brightness of the sun and moon above had been permanently eclipsed, while down below the rivers and streams had lost their power. Good and honest people are ignored, while spineless flatterers are exalted. The quiet calm of natural action has been cast aside, in favour of perpetual argument and conflict. What nonsense human beings are making of their lives.

10

Innate virtue

I believe in allowing the world to follow its own path, and not interfering; but I disapprove of any attempt to try and control the world.

You should let the world be as it wants to be; any interference will deface it. The world has its own innate virtue; so if you change the world, you will corrupt it. If nothing under heaven is distorted, then the world will remain innocent and pure. So why should anyone want to control the world?

There was a time when rulers did not interfere with the world. All men, women and children were allowed to live in their own way, and so everyone was happy. All living beings were allowed to live in their own way, so they too were happy. No one felt frustrated or oppressed. But then rulers appeared who were intent on changing things according to their own ideas and visions. As a result happiness turned to misery; men, women, children, and all living beings, became prone to diseases, of both the body and the mind.

If misery is present, virtue is absent. And if virtue is absent, disease and death are imminent.

11

Symptons of corruption

Do people strive to be cheerful, beyond what is natural? If so, they harm the yang. Are people too angry and vengeful? If so, they harm the yin. If both yin and yang are corrupted, then the mind and the body will become unbalanced, causing all kinds of pain and illness. People will find themselves unable to control their emotions, and they will react to situations in peculiar ways. They will feel restless, constantly wanting to move about, but not knowing what to do. They will make plans and devise plots, but with no purpose. They will become ambitious, wanting power and wealth for their own sake; and so the world will soon be thrown into turmoil.

When yin and yang are corrupted, people are no longer content with the gentle colours of nature; they want to stimulate their eyes with brighter, harsher colours. They are no longer content with the gentle sounds of nature; they want to stimulate their ears with louder, harsher sounds. They are no longer content with the virtue of nature; they want to stimulate their imaginations with grand schemes. They are no longer content with the harmony of nature; they want to stimulate their souls with elaborate religious rituals. They are no longer content with simple friendship; they want to stimulate their emotions with complex codes of behaviour. They are no longer content with knowing what they need to know; they want to stimulate their minds with all kinds of speculation.

11

The human soul

Take care how you play with people's souls. People's souls should not be pushed down or pulled up; pushing and pulling the soul causes either profound melancholy or uncontrollable rage. Be gentle with people's souls, allowing them to remain as they are.

The human soul at times can be soft and generous, and at times can be harsh and mean. The human soul at times can be tough, able to withstand any kind of attack, and at times can be vulnerable. The human soul at times can be as hot as a blazing fire, and at times can be as cold as ice. The human soul at times can be so swift that, in the moment it takes to nod the head, it has travelled across the world and back; and at times it can be slow. When it is at rest, the human soul can be as deep and dark as the bed of the ocean; when it is active, the human soul can be as high and bright as the largest star.

When anyone seeks to bind the human soul, it races away – for it is the nature of the human soul to be free.

11

Inactivity and activity

Wise people contemplate heaven, but they do not assist it.
They wish to be virtuous, but do not allow thoughts of virtue
to encumber them. They strive to follow the Way, but they
do not make plans. They are kind to others, but never try to
change them. They make no effort to be righteous, but act
naturally in a righteous manner. They do what needs to be
done without complaint or resentment. They make rules for
themselves, but never impose those rules on others. They
value their relatives and friends, but never use friends and
relatives for their own advantage. They take care of their possessions, but are happy to share them with others.

What is the Way? There is the Way of heaven, and there
is the Way of humanity. The Way of heaven is to be inactive;
the Way of humanity is to be active. The Way of heaven is
the ruler, and the Way of earth is the servant. Inactivity and
activity may seem quite different; but if the former rules the
latter, they are one and the same. Reflect on this day by day.

11

Fulfilling potential

The Way is deep in its profundity, quiet in its tranquillity, and pure in its clarity. Without the Way gold would not glisten, and stones would not be hard. Gold has the potential to glisten; but if the light of the Way did not shine within it, then it would be dull. Stones have the potential to be hard; but if the strength of the Way did not assert itself within them, then they would be soft. Every object and every living being depends on the Way; and through the Way their potential is fulfilled.

Men and women of wisdom know their own potential – and that their potential can only be fulfilled by following the Way. Like gold the body is potentially radiant with health; but without the Way it is wracked by disease. Like stones the body is potentially strong; but without the Way it is limp and weak.

Men and women of wisdom can see in the darkness of ignorance, and hear in the silence of stupidity.

12

The old man and his jar

Kung, a famous spiritual teacher, was walking beside a river, when he saw an old man working on his land. The man had prepared a field for planting, and was irrigating it with a small jar; time after time he dipped the jar in his well, walked to his field, and poured out the water. He was huffing and puffing with exhaustion, yet only a tiny portion of the ground was wet. Kung went up to the old man, and said: 'There is a machine that can irrigate a hundred fields in a single day. Wouldn't you like to have one?' 'How does such a machine work?' the old man asked. Kung explained its elaborate mechanism.

The old man was furious. Then he laughed, and said: 'I have been told that all machines go wrong; and when a machine goes wrong, the mind becomes anxious and upset; when the mind is anxious and upset, it loses its purity and simplicity; and without purity and simplicity of mind it is impossible to follow the Way. So I refuse to use a machine.'

Kung looked bewildered. Seeing Kung's expression, the old man asked: 'Are you the kind of person that seeks knowledge in order to appear wise? Are you the sort that composes poems in order to become famous?' Kung did not reply, and wandered away, his face white with confusion.

Discovery of virtue

When Kung returned home, his followers noticed that he looked bewildered, and asked him the reason. He replied: 'Previously I thought that every person should be active, that every action should have a purpose, and that success in fulfilling its purpose was the standard by which an action should be judged. In short, my teaching was that people should use the minimum of effort to achieve the maximum results. But now I no longer believe this.'

His followers asked what he now believed. Kung said: 'Virtue consists in following the Way. People following the Way become whole in body; and as they become whole in body, they also become whole in mind. They live side by side with people not following the Way, and do many of the same things; but they make no distinction between success and failure. Their simplicity is astonishing. They have no interest in machines to ease their labours, or in profits as a reward for their labours. They do not go where their soul does not take them, and they do not do what their soul does not prompt them to do. They are indifferent to praise and blame; even if the whole world were to acclaim them or disparage them, they would pay no attention. They are utterly calm, and nothing can perturb them. Yes, such people possess real virtue; and by comparison I am just a wave on the sea blown by the wind.'

Service and sycophancy

When your children have grown to adulthood, you may wish them to indulge your every whim and desire; but such indulgence would not truly serve you. You may wish them to agree with everything you say; but such flattery would not truly serve you. The worthy son or daughter cares for you according to your needs, not your wants, and speaks to you honestly, and not submissively.

In the same way a ruler may wish his ministers to obey his every command without question, and to gasp with wonder at his every utterance. But such sycophancy would not truly serve him. On the contrary, the good minister has the courage to question the ruler's judgement, and to offer wise advice, even at the risk of incurring the ruler's wrath.

Yet the world refuses to grasp these truths, and insists on confusing service with sycophancy. Children are praised for always agreeing with their parents, and for finding turns of phrase that will please their parents. And the skill that is most likely to advance a man's career, is the ability to ingratiate himself with his superiors.

12

Doves in a cage

There are five ways in which people may lose their innate virtue. The first is when the various colours confuse the eye, and deprive it of clarity of vision. The second is when the various sounds confuse the ear, and deprive it of clarity of hearing. The third is when the various smells confuse the nose, and cause pain in the forehead. The fourth is when the various flavours deaden the palate, and deprive it of taste. The fifth is when excessive pleasure unsettles the soul, and makes the emotions unstable.

These five ways of losing innate virtue bring great trouble. There are teachers, calling themselves wise, who actually want people to lose their innate virtue. They want people to see images and listen to music that will confuse them. They want people to wear brightly coloured robes, to eat spicy food at every meal, and to cover themselves with perfumes at all times. They teach that all this brings happiness. But if people follow their teaching, they are like doves flying into a cage, and locking the door behind them.

12

Heaven's Way

It is heaven's Way to journey, and yet to gather no moss; by this means all forms of life are brought to perfection. The true king journeys, and yet gathers no moss; by this means the whole world comes to his feet. Wise people journey, and yet gather no moss; by this means even the fish in the ocean revere them.

To understand heaven clearly, to grasp the teaching of the wise, to comprehend the magnificence of the universe, to lead a life of virtue, and to act with genuine spontaneity — that is the nature of people who follow the Way. They seem to know nothing, and yet they discern everything. They seem to do nothing, and yet they possess the world.

13

The still soul

Wise people are still and tranquil. This is not because they see any value in being still and tranquil; it is simply that wisdom induces this state. No one can perturb them. Even if every living being gathered around a truly wise person, and shouted and screamed, the wise person would remain calm.

When it is still, water gives such a perfect reflection that you can even see your own eyebrows within it. When water is still, the carpenter can set his level perfectly by it. If still water offers such perfection, think what a still soul can offer! Heaven and earth are reflected in it; it is a mirror of all life. In its lack of movement it reflects all movement. In its inaction it reflects all action. By going nowhere it reflects the birds flying across the sky from one continent to another.

The still soul discerns everything, but passes judgement on nothing. The still soul is always generous, but never righteous. The still soul ages without growing old, because it does nothing to exhaust itself. To possess a still soul is to be truly happy.

13

Agreeing with everything

A man called Shi travelled for many days, over mountains and through deserts, in order to visit a famous spiritual teacher. When he arrived, he found the teacher living alone, with the teacher's sister and her family living nearby. Shi was shocked, and said to the teacher: 'If you were as wise and good as people say you are, you would be happy to have your sister living with you. Yet you have thrown her out of your house, and forced her and her family to build themselves another house. How foolish and selfish you are!' The teacher showed no emotion, and said nothing. Shi turned his back, and walked away in disgust.

The following day Shi returned, and said to the teacher: 'Yesterday I was rude to you. But today the urge to be rude has gone. Why is this?' The teacher replied: 'I have freed myself from any desire to be wise. If you had said that I was an ox, I should have agreed with you. If you had said I was a horse, I should have agreed with you. People are constantly making assertions; and this provokes others to contradict them. Since I have no desire to be wise, I neither make assertions, nor contradict them.'

Shi shrank back, so that even the teacher's shadow could not touch him. Then he knelt down, crawled forward, and asked the teacher to free him from all desire for wisdom. The teacher replied: 'Your face is ugly, your eyes glare, your mouth hangs open, and your manner is pompous. All this makes me distrust you.'

Perfect people

Shi was shocked at the teacher's insults; but he restrained himself, so he showed no emotion and said nothing.

The teacher continued: 'The Way is not frightened by that which is vast and strong; nor does it despise that which is small and weak. All life comes from the Way. The Way is so immense that it encompasses all that exists; it is so deep that it can never be fathomed. Only perfect people can understand this. Perfect people are the true leaders of humanity – a daunting task. But they do not feel trapped by the task, nor are they flattered by the honour. They hold the reins of power over the entire world, but this gives them no personal pleasure. Their discernment uncovers all falsehood, but they have no thought of personal gain. Their minds quickly reach the heart of every problem and issue that arises, and they know how to uphold the truth. Their spirits are never weary, because they travel with the Tao. Since they are completely virtuous, they have no need of righteousness or religion; perfect people have their souls set on what is right.'

The aristocrat and the wheelwright

A wealthy aristocrat was sitting in his hall reading a book. Outside in the courtyard a wheelwright called Pien was making a wheel. Pien put down his hammer and chisel, and went to see the aristocrat.

'What are you reading?' Pien asked. 'The writings of a very wise man,' the aristocrat replied. 'Is he still living?' Pien asked. 'No, he died long ago,' the aristocrat replied. 'Then this book is nothing but the rubbish left over from the past,' the wheelwright declared. The aristocrat was furious, and exclaimed: 'How dare you comment on what I choose to read! If you can justify your remark, you shall live; if not, you shall die.'

Pien said: 'I look at the matter from the perspective of my own work. If I use my hammer too softly, it may make a pleasant sound, but it does not make a good wheel. If I use my hammer too vigorously, I soon become tired, and have to stop. So, as I grasp the hammer in my hand, I also hold it in my soul. I cannot explain this process; I just know it. This means that I cannot explain it to other people, even my own son; he must learn it for himself. And when I die, I shall take my knowledge with me. It is the same with the wise people of the past; when they die, they take their wisdom with them. That is why I call your book rubbish left over from the past.'

13

Doing nothing and creating everything

Does heaven move and the earth stand still? Do the sun and the moon argue about where to go? Who is master of all this? Who controls it, and holds all its disparate parts together? Who, by doing nothing, makes everything happen?

Is there some hidden cause that makes things as they are, regardless of their wishes? Or does everything move and turn at random? Do clouds come before rain, or does rain cause clouds? And what causes both clouds and rain to exist? Who, by doing nothing, brings all this joyful abundance into being?

The winds come from the north; then they turn west; and then they turn east. They swirl up into the sky. But where do they go? Whose breath are they? Who, by doing nothing, creates all this activity?

Benevolence and virtue

The chief minister asked Chuang Tzu: 'Does virtue consist in benevolence?'. Chuang Tzu replied: 'Even wolves and tigers are benevolent.' 'What do you mean?' the chief minister asked. Chuang Tzu replied: 'Parents care for their offspring; that is benevolence.'

'So if virtue does not consist in benevolence, in what does it consist?' the chief minister asked. 'Virtue is not the same as affection,' Chuang Tzu said. The chief minister replied: 'I have heard it said that without affection there is no love, and that without love children will not honour their parents. How can virtue exist without children honouring their parents?'

Chuang Tzu said: 'Virtue belongs to a far higher order than the honouring of parents. It is easy for me to forget my parents, but hard to make my parents forget me. It is easy for me to forget the world, but hard to make the world forget me. I attain virtue when the world has no cause to remember me.'

The chief minister asked Chuang Tzu to make himself clearer. Chuang Tzu continued: 'Honouring parents, mutual respect, benevolence, righteousness, loyalty, integrity, valour – all these may be valuable in their context, but they are not virtue. Disregard for worldly status, indifference to wealth, unconcern with fame and praise – these are the signs of virtue.'

14

Knowledge and wisdom

Scholars, who have devoted their lives to the accumulation of knowledge, tend to be haughty and arrogant, regarding themselves as superior to the common people. They like to formulate great theories, and they are critical and disparaging of those whose minds cannot grasp these theories. They preach to the common people about benevolence, righteousness, loyalty and valour; and they instruct them to be humble, moderate and courteous. They enjoy speaking about their own intellectual achievements, and relish the fame that these achievements bring them. They take pleasure in arranging and presiding over religious rituals that important people attend. And they puff up with pride when rulers seek their advice.

Those following the Way like to live in remote and isolated places. They take pleasure in the natural beauty of lakes and forests, and the rhythmic sound of waves breaking on a beach is music to their ears. They never hurry, but remain always calm. They take regular physical exercise to maintain the body's strength and to refresh the mind. They have no power, yet they rule the world. They have no wealth, but they possess everything. They have no purpose, yet they attain perfect virtue. They know nothing, but they are supremely wise.

Harmony with heaven

Serenity, detachment, tranquillity, action without action —
these are the qualities that come from following the Way.
Wise people, who follow the Way, are at rest; nothing can
disturb their peace of mind.

The lives of wise people are a manifestation of heaven.
When they are still, they are like yin; when they are moving,
they are like yang. They bring neither good fortune nor bad.
They ignore knowledge, and are never nostalgic. In life they
float, and in death they rest. They do not devise schemes nor
do they make plans; they accept whatever exists and whatever
occurs. They shine, but are not seen. They pass no judgements, and keep no record of rights and wrongs. They are in
harmony with heaven's virtue.

It is sad that sadness and happiness are corruptions of
virtue; that joy and anger are contrary to the Way; that good
and evil have no connection with wisdom. So for the soul to
be free from sadness and happiness, virtue must be perfect.
For the soul to be free from joy and anger, the Way must be
followed. For the soul to transcend good and evil, wisdom
must be profound.

To be changeless is to be perfectly still. To provoke no
opposition is to be empty. To have no feelings of dissent is
to be pure.

If the body is overworked and has no rest, it collapses. In
the same way, if the mind and soul are continuously active,
they collapse.

Purity, serenity and freedom

Water, if other things are not mixed with it, is clear; if it is not stirred up, it is level; and, if nothing blocks its passage, it flows freely from a higher to a lower level. This is like the virtue of heaven. If you wish to be clear and pure, nothing should be allowed to contaminate you. If you wish to be level and serene, nothing should be allowed to stir you up. To move freely towards the deepest understanding, nothing should be allowed to impede you.

The Way consists in utter purity, serenity and freedom. Ordinary people aspire towards wealth; scholars crave fame; rulers want power. But the desire for wealth contaminates the soul; the desire for fame stirs up the soul; and the desire for power blocks the soul. Therefore followers of the Way are utterly indifferent to wealth, fame and power.

15

Timely action

In the distant past our ancestors were careful not to disturb the harmony of nature. They did not use their intelligence and knowledge to disrupt the world. On the contrary they acted only according to nature's own laws. What could be better than this?

The Way has no place for greed, because greed prompts people to disrupt nature. Greed is the enemy of virtue.

Our ancestors spoke of timeliness of action. By this they meant that the same action may be virtuous or not virtuous, according to the moment at which it is performed. If an action is timely, it is in harmony with nature; if it is untimely, it is out of harmony with nature.

The Way has no place for official carriages and badges of office. People aspiring to such things will always act in an untimely manner.

16

The great ocean

You cannot discuss the ocean with a frog living in a well; its understanding is limited by the space in which it lives. You cannot discuss ice with a summer insect; its understanding is limited by the season in which it lives. You cannot discuss the Way with a scholar who has devoted his life to the acquisition of knowledge; his understanding is limited by his knowledge. When you come out of your well, and see the great ocean, you will realize how small-minded you have been.

Of all the waters in the world, none is so great as the ocean. Ten thousand rivers flow into it, yet it is never full. The seasons of the year come and go, but the ocean remains unchanged. On land there may be floods or droughts, but the ocean takes no notice. It is so much greater than even the mightiest river, that it is impossible to measure the difference.

I take my place on earth, and receive breath from yin and yang. If heaven is a great tree, then I am a tiny stone on the ground beneath. If heaven is a great mountain, I am a shrub perched on its slopes. Knowing my own smallness, I am free from pride.

Not judging

Wise people look at small things, and do not regard them as paltry; they look at large things, and do not regard them as unwieldy. In short, they do not judge things by their size.

Wise people look at the past, and do not find it tedious; they look at the present, and do not regard it as exciting. In short, they do not judge things by their place in the course of history.

Wise people look at things that are full, and do not take delight in what they see; they look at things that are empty, and do not despise their emptiness. In short, they do not judge things by measuring them.

Wise people look at life, and do not try to cling on to it; they look at death, and do not try to push it away. In short, they do not judge the world by their own existence.

17

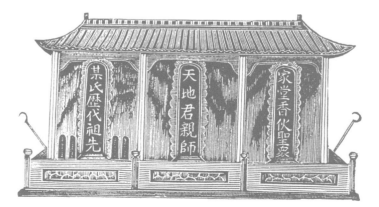

The measure of ignorance

Calculate what you know, and compare it with what you do not know; that which you do not know, far exceeds that which you do know. Calculate the time that you have been alive, and compare it with the time before you were born; the time before your birth far exceeds the time since your birth. This reminds you of how small and insignificant you are. If you think you are important, then you are muddled and confused, and will never do anything important.

Do you think that the tip of a hair is a measure of the smallest thing that exists? Do you think that heaven and earth are big enough to contain the largest thing that exists? In truth none of us can measure the smallest or the largest thing – that is a measure of our ignorance.

For the smallest thing in existence the largest thing is far too large to conceive. For the largest thing in existence the smallest thing is far too small to conceive. But largeness only has meaning in relation to smallness, and smallness only has meaning in relation to largeness. This shows the limits of our understanding.

17

No harm

Wise people do not harm others, nor do they make any show of benevolence or righteousness. They do nothing for the sake of personal profit, and they despise no one, even the humblest beggar. They make no effort to accumulate wealth or goods, nor do they make any show of giving things away or of refusing what is offered to them. They do not seek the help of others in their work; but they make no show of being self-sufficient, nor do they pass judgement on those who are greedy and corrupt. Their actions differ from those of the mass of people, but they make no show of being unusual or special. They are content to mix with the crowd, but they do not hold in contempt those who push themselves forward.

Wise people are not influenced by offers of grand titles or large stipends; nor are they influenced by threats of punishments and disgrace. They know that no line can be drawn between right and wrong. They seek neither fame nor gain, but accept things as they are.

17

Size, function and judgement

If we regard a thing as big, because it possesses a certain quality of bigness, then we may find that same quality in everything else. If we regard a thing as small, because it possesses a certain quality of smallness, then we may find that same quality in everything else. If we know that heaven and earth are tiny grains, and that the tip of a hair is a range of mountains, then we have understood the nature of size.

If we regard a thing as useful, because we can think of a use for it, then we shall find the same quality in everything else. If we regard a thing as useless, because we can think of no use for it, then we shall find that same quality in everything else. If we know that east and west are opposite, but depend on one another, then we have understood the nature of function.

If we regard a thing as right, because it conforms to some standard of rightness, then we shall find that everything conforms to some standard of rightness. If we regard a thing as wrong, because it is contrary to some standard of rightness, then we shall find that everything fails to conform to some standard. If we know that in every dispute both parties are convinced of their rightness, then we have understood the nature of moral judgements.

17

The principle of heaven and earth

A beam or pillar can be used to batter down a city wall, but it is useless for blocking a small hole. A thoroughbred horse can gallop a vast distance; but when it comes to catching rats, it is no match for a weasel. The horned owl can catch fleas at night, and can spot the tip of a hair in pitch darkness; but when daylight comes, no matter how wide it opens its eyes, it cannot even see a mountain.

Do you say that you will make righteousness your master, and do away with wrong? Do you say that you will make order your master, and do away with disorder? If so, you have not understood the principle of heaven and earth. It is like saying that you will make heaven your master, and do away with earth. Or like saying that you will make yin your master, and do away with yang. Those talking in this way are either fools or liars.

17

The gallop of life

Do not cramp or constrain your will, as that would cause you to depart from the Way. Do not strive for consistency in your actions, as that would cause you to lose sight of the Way. Be firm with yourself, never making excuses for your short-comings. Be gentle with yourself, never demanding of yourself more than you can give. Let your mind be as open to the ideas of others, as a field without hedges is open to the four winds.

All living beings are born and die; you cannot depend upon them. All events start and finish; you cannot depend upon them. The years cannot be held back; time cannot be stopped. Growth and decay, fullness and emptiness, birth and death – the rhythm of change cannot be halted. Life passes at a gallop; it is like a headlong dash towards death. With every moment and every movement your body ages. What should you do and not do to prevent ageing? Nothing.

Yet if you follow the Way, and thence acquire perfect virtue, fire will not be able to burn you, water will not be able to drown you, cold and heat will not be able to dis-comfort you, and wild beasts will not be able to injure you. This is because you will be indifferent to fortune and mis-fortune, good and bad.

17

The millipede, the snake and the wind

The millipede envies the snake, and the snake envies the wind.

The millipede said to the snake: 'I have all these legs to help me move along, and you have no legs; yet I cannot keep up with you.' The snake replied: 'I cannot change the way I am. What should I do with legs if I had them?'

The snake said to the wind: 'I move my body from side to side to help me move along, and you have no body; yet I cannot keep up with you.' The wind replied: 'If you hold up a finger against me, you force me to divert from my course. Yet I can push down trees and blow over grand houses. So I ignore all the little defeats, and concentrate on the great victories. That is my wisdom.'

17

The frog and the turtle

Have you heard of the frog in the well? A giant turtle, who lived in the great ocean, came to visit the well. He looked over the side, and introduced himself to the frog. The frog said: 'What fun I have in this well! The stones above the water have lots of little ledges, and I can hop between them. If I become hot, I can dive into the water and have a bath. There are all kinds of little insects flying about, which I can capture in my mouth and eat. I am the complete master of my well. Come inside and share my pleasure.'

But when the turtle lifted its left foot into the well, its right knee became wedged; so it drew back, complaining that the well was too small. Then it said: 'Let me tell you about my home, which is the ocean. It's so wide that no one can measure its width. It's so deep that no one can measure its depth. When the rain falls, it never rises; when there is a drought, it never falls. It never changes, whether for an instant or forever.'

The frog was dumbfounded – and from that moment it ceased to enjoy its life in the well, and was perpetually discontent.

17

The sacred tortoise

Once, when Chuang Tzu was fishing in a river, the king sent two officials to invite him to come and administer the kingdom.

Chuang Tzu, without turning his head, replied: 'I have heard that the king owns a sacred tortoise; it died three thousand years ago, and the king keeps it in a box, and stores it in his ancestral temple. Would this tortoise rather be dead, and have its bones worshipped; or would it rather be alive and dragging its feet in the mud?' The officials replied: 'It would rather be dragging its feet in the mud.' Chuang Tzu: 'I am the same. So go away.'

17

Knowing fish

Chuang Tzu was strolling along a river with a friend. Chuang Tzu said to the friend: 'Look how the fish dart about in the water as they please. That is what fish really enjoy.' The friend replied: 'You're not a fish. So how do you know what fish enjoy?' Chuang Tzu retorted: 'You're not me. So how do you know that I don't know what fish enjoy?' The friend said: 'I'm not you, so I certainly don't know what you know. On the other hand, you're not a fish; so that still proves you don't know what fish enjoy.'

Chuang Tzu said: 'Let's go back to your original question. You asked me how I know what fish enjoy; you did not ask me whether I know what fish enjoy. So in fact you already knew that I know what fish enjoy.'

17

The world's values

Is there such a thing as supreme happiness in the world, or
is there not? Is there some way to prolong your life, or is
there not? What should you do? What should you avoid?
What rules should you follow? What should you love and
what should you hate?

These are what the world values: wealth, power, and status. These are what the world regards as the sources of happiness: rich food, fine clothes, beautiful sights, and sweet
sounds. These are what the world despises: poverty, lowliness
and disgrace. These are what the world regards as the sources
of misery: poor food, rags, ugly sights, and ugly sounds.

Rich people rush round in their efforts to acquire wealth,
and accumulate far more than they could possibly need. This
is a foolish way to treat the body. Powerful people spend
their days and nights devising schemes to enhance their
power. This too is a foolish way to treat the body. Eminent
people are constantly anxious that people will not accord
them sufficient respect. This too is a foolish way to treat the
body.

People striving to serve others are regarded by the world
as good. But their goodness does not prolong their lives.

18

Purity and peace

I look at the ways in which ordinary people seek happiness.
I look at the things for which they strive, and which they say
bring happiness. Yet I am not convinced their happiness is
real. Certainly I should not find happiness in those things.
Does happiness really exist?

I regard inaction as happiness, and yet ordinary people are
frightened of inaction, complaining that it makes them bored.
I say that the highest happiness is no happiness, and the highest praise is no praise. The world cannot decide what is right
and wrong; people constantly argue about this. But inaction
rises above this distinction.

Let me put it this way. The inaction of heaven is its purity, and the inaction of earth is its peace. Let purity combine
with peace, and there is perfection. So from inaction comes
perfection.

18

Weeping and singing

Chuang Tzu's wife died. His friend Hui came to convey his condolences. He found Chuang Tzu sitting with his legs sprawled out, beating on a drum, and singing. Hui was shocked, and remonstrated: 'You lived with her for many decades, and she brought up your children. I should understand if by now you had overcome your tears. But how can you bring yourself to beat a drum and sing? You are going too far.'

Chuang Tzu replied: 'You are wrong. When she died, do you not think I felt grief, as anyone would? But then I looked back to the time of her birth. Then I looked back to the time before her birth, when she did not have a body. Then I looked back at the time before that, when she did not have a spirit. After reflecting on all this, I began to look forward again: to the mysterious process by which she acquired a spirit; to the mysterious process by which she acquired a body; to the mysterious process by which she was born. Then I realized that at death another mysterious process has occurred. These thoughts led me to see her progress through time as like the passing of the seasons. So I stopped weeping and began singing.'

18

Feelings about death

An old man and a young man were on a journey. Suddenly a tumour appeared on the old man's elbow. The old man was startled. When he had looked closely at the tumour, he declared: 'This is a sign of a fatal disease that is consuming my body. Soon I shall be dead.'

'Do you resent your imminent death?' the young man asked. The old man said: 'I have no reason for resentment. In order to live, we borrow the energy of life. Death occurs when the loan is withdrawn. So rather than resenting death, I am grateful for every moment of life.'

'Are you frightened of your imminent death?' the young man asked.' The old man said: 'I have no reason for fear. Birth is one process of change, and death is another. I coped with birth quite adequately, so I shall cope with death in the same way.'

18

The testimony of a skull

Chuang Tzu was on a journey, and came across an old skull. He poked it with his stick, and said to it: 'Were you so greedy for wealth that you lost all caution – and so came to this? Were you a great king who was overthrown, and then executed by your usurper? Did you commit some crime for which you were hanged in this remote spot, bringing disgrace on your family? Were you so poor that you could not afford food, and so starved to death?'

The sun was falling below the horizon. So Chuang Tzu lay down to sleep, with the skull as his pillow. In the middle of the night the skull spoke to him in a dream: 'You talk foolish nonsense – as does everyone entangled by life. The dead have a quite different attitude. Would you like me to tell you about the dead?' 'Yes,' answered Chuang Tzu. The skull continued: 'Amongst the dead there are no rulers and no subjects; there is no wealth and poverty; there is no honour and disgrace; there is no right and wrong; there is no pleasure and pain. Even the mightiest king could not be as happy as the dead are.'

Chuang Tzu could not believe this, and said: 'If your bones could be knit together again to form a living body, and if you could return to your family, would you not want that?' The skull frowned, and said: 'Why should I take on the troubles of being a human again?'

18

The bird in the temple

One day a beautiful bird flew into the garden of the king's palace, and perched on one of the trees. The king saw it, and was enchanted by its appearance. He ordered his servants to capture it in a net and put it in his ancestral temple. There the king arranged for his chefs to prepare the finest food for it, and his musicians to play their sweetest music for its entertainment. But the food made the bird sick, and the music made its head spin; so three days later it died.

Would you like a royal bird to capture you, feed you with bird food, and sing birdsong in your ear all day? The royal bird might imagine it was being kind, but in truth it would kill you. If you truly love a bird, allow it to live like a bird, eating the food and hearing the sounds that are natural to it.

Fish thrive in the water; if you bring them onto the land, they quickly die. But human beings thrive on land; put them in the water, and they quickly die. Let every creature live according to its nature.

The skull in the undergrowth

Chuang-Tzu was on a journey, and sat down at the side of the lane for a rest. He spotted in the undergrowth a skull; so he pulled it out, and saw it was at least a hundred years old.

He held it up, and spoke to it: 'You and I know that you have never really died, and that you never really lived. Does this distress you? Am I really enjoying myself?'

18

Good health

If you have understood the true nature of life, you do not try to make life something different from what it is. If you have grasped the true nature of destiny, you do not try to influence the course of life through ingenious schemes.

If you wish to sustain your body in good health, take care of the world. Your body is part of the world; so you cannot abuse the world, and still expect your body to remain well.

By treating the world well, you can be at peace with it. By being at peace with the world, you can be calm. By being calm, you can follow the Way.

19

The original breath

Perfect people can walk under water without drowning, and can walk through fire without burning. How can they do this? They can do it because they guard the original breath within them. This has nothing to do with intelligence, skill, determination, or courage.

Everything has a shape, a colour, a sound, a texture, and a fragrance. These are the outward appearances that separate one thing from another. Yet everything arises from that which has no shape, colour, sound, texture, or fragrance. If you understand this, and understand it fully, nothing can harm you or impede you. You live within limits that have no limit; you live within boundaries that have no beginning and end; you breathe the original breath, and act without effort. In short, you are perfect.

19

The drunkard falling from a carriage

If a sober man falls from a carriage, he is likely to be injured and even killed. He is aware of what is happening, and so is stiff with fear; this stiffness causes his body to be hurt as it hits the ground.

If a drunken man falls from a carriage, even though the carriage may be moving fast, he is likely to escape injury. He has the same flesh and bones as the sober man. Yet he is unaware of what is happening, so his body remains supple and relaxed; as a result he easily absorbs the impact of the fall.

If you can keep yourself whole by means of wine, how much better will you be able to keep yourself whole by means of heaven. A man who is in harmony with heaven, can never be harmed.

Do not try to do what is natural to you, because you will always fail. Do what is natural to heaven. Those who do what is natural to heaven, also do what is natural to themselves. Those who reject what is natural to heaven, harm themselves.

Catching insects

Chuang Tzu once passed through a forest, where he saw a man whose back was bent almost double. Despite his disability the man was catching cicada insects with a sticky pole, as easily as though he were grabbing them with his hand. Chuang Tzu exclaimed: 'What skill you have! How have you acquired it?'

The man replied: 'For six months I practised balancing two balls on top of each other on the end of the pole. Then for another six months I practised balancing three balls on top of each other on the end of the pole. Then for another six months I practised balancing four balls on top of each other on the end of the pole. Then for another six months I practised balancing five balls on top of each other on the end of the pole. By now I was satisfied that I had the ability to catch cicadas as easily as if I were grabbing them with my hand. But still I was not ready. I spent a further six months learning to hold my body as still as if it were a tree trunk. And I spent a further six months learning to concentrate my mind, so I should be aware of nothing but cicadas. I was now confident that I could not fail.'

Chuang Tzu thanked the man, and left. He frequently repeated the man's words to others, and concluded: 'If the mind and the body are directed to a single object, then that object will be attained.'

The skill of the ferryman

A man called Hui was once on a ferry, and noticed that the ferryman handled the boat with supreme skill. Hui asked the ferryman: 'Can one study how to handle a boat?' The ferryman replied: 'A good swimmer will learn very quickly. And someone who can swim under water, and who has never seen a boat before, will know immediately.' Hui was baffled, and asked the ferryman to explain himself; but the ferryman could not.

Later Hui went to Chuang Tzu, related the ferryman's words, and asked if he could explain them. Chuang Tzu said: 'A good swimmer will learn very quickly – that is because he knows how to ignore the water. Someone who can swim under water, and who has never seen a boat before, will know immediately – that is because he regards the water as if it were dry land, and the overturning of a boat as if were a wagon turning over. So nothing can disturb his inner calm.'

Chuang Tzu continued: 'Consider archery, in which you excel. If you are shooting for pleasure, you hit your target without effort. But if you are shooting for high stakes, you start to worry about your aim – then you are likely to miss. When you lose your inner calm, you lose your skill as well.'

19

Internal and external

There was a man called Po, who dwelt in a cave, drank only pure water from a nearby stream, and never sought wealth. He lived in this manner for seventy years, and still had the complexion of a child. Then one day a hungry tiger came past, and ate him up.

The was a man called Yi, who loved to visit grand houses, eat rich food and drink fine wine. He lived in this manner for forty years. Then a fever developed within his belly, and he died.

So let us compare these two men. Po took care of what is internal; but the tiger came from outside, and killed him. Yi concerned himself with what is external, but the fever attacked him from within, and killed him. This suggests there is a middle way, in which the wise person looks after both what is internal and what is external.

19

True danger

When a traveller has been killed by robbers on a certain road, people become anxious about the safety of that road. Fathers warn sons, and elder brothers warn younger brothers, not to travel along that road without an armed guard. That is wise, is it not?

Yet there are things that are far more dangerous than travelling along a road infested with robbers. If you allow your mind to fill with corrupt thoughts, or allow your soul to fill with corrupt feelings, you put your eternal existence in danger. So lying in bed day-dreaming can be the most dangerous of all activities.

19

The diver in the waterfall

Hui went to visit a famous waterfall. He watched with amaze-
ment the water falling from a great height, and then forming
a cauldron of white foam at the bottom. While he was staring at the waterfall, a young man dived into the white foam.
Hui saw this out of the corner of his eye, and assumed that
the man had fallen into the foam by accident. So he stood on
the bank, ready to pull him out of the foam, and save his life.

But a few minutes later the young man emerged from the
water some distance downstream, calmly pulled himself onto
the bank, and strolled back to the waterfall. At first Hui
thought he must be a ghost; but as the man came closer, he
realized he was real.

'Do you have some special way of keeping afloat in the
water?' Hui asked. The man replied: 'I have no special way.
I simply follow the water. So I go under with the swirls,
and come up with the eddies. I never think about myself.
That is how I stay afloat.' 'Would I stay afloat if I didn't
think about myself?' Hui asked. The young man replied:
'You have always lived on dry land. So as you walk along,
you don't think about yourself; that's how you stay upright.
I have always dived in and out of the water. Do not try to
be what you are not.'

19

The beautiful bell-stand

A woodworker called Ching carved a beautiful bell-stand. Everyone marvelled at it. When the king saw it, he asked Ching: 'What art do you possess, that enables you to carve so beautifully?'

Ching replied: 'I am merely a craftsman. When I am making a bell-stand, I begin by fasting, in order to still my mind. When I have fasted for three days, I no longer have any thoughts of praise or congratulations for my work. When I have fasted for five days, I am no longer concerned whether I am skilful or clumsy. When I have fasted for seven days, I forget that I have four limbs and a body; I forget even that I live in a country ruled by a king. After that I go to the forest high up on the mountain, and examine the nature of trees. Eventually I find a tree in which I can see the bell-stand already present. I chop down the tree, and allow my hands to carve out the bell-stand. So you see I have no art; I am a craftsman who reveals the art of nature.'

Forgetting your feet

You forget your feet when your shoes are comfortable; you only remember your feet when your shoes pinch. You forget your waist when your belt is comfortable; you only remember your waist when your belt is too tight. You forget right and wrong when your conscience is clear; you only remember right and wrong when your conscience is troubled. You forget that with which you are in harmony; you remember only that with which you are out of harmony.

If you are truly following the Way, you forget about it; you only remember the Way when you have strayed from it.

19

Human food for a bird

A man called Sun called to see Chuang Tzu, and said: 'When I was a child, no one ever said I behaved badly. But since I have been adult, my life has been disastrous. First I became a farmer, and never had a good harvest. Then I served the king, and was never promoted. Now I am utterly miserable. What have I done to deserve such a fate?'

Chuang Tzu replied: 'If you had been perfect, you would have had no concern for the results of your efforts. So you would have accepted whatever harvest the land produced. And you would have accepted whatever position the king gave you. By this means, far from being miserable, you would have been contented and happy.' Sun said nothing, and went away.

That evening Chuang Tzu kept sighing. 'Why are you sighing?' one of his disciples asked. Chuang Tzu said: 'My words will have hindered Sun, not helped him. He was a bird, and I gave him human food.'

19

The knotted tree and the cackling goose

Chuang Tzu was walking with a disciple through a forest, when they came across a very ancient tree. 'How has that tree survived so long?' the disciple asked. Chuang Tzu replied: 'Its wood is so twisted and knotted that it is completely useless; any object made from its wood would immediately fall apart. So no woodcutter has even bothered to chop it down. Its uselessness is its protection.'

That evening they reached a friend's house. The friend said: 'I wish to cook a goose for your dinner. I have two geese: one cackles whenever strangers appear, and so gives us a valuable warning; the other remains silent. Which goose shall I kill?' Chuang Tzu said: 'Obviously you must kill the silent goose.'

The following morning the disciple said to Chuang Tzu: 'Yesterday we came across a tree which had survived because it was useless. Then we ate a goose that was killed because it was useless, while another goose survived because it was useful. So is it best to be useful or useless?' Chuang Tzu laughed, and said: 'The art of life is to know when to be useless, and when to be useful.'

20

Advice to an anxious ruler

A wealthy ruler came to see Chuang Tzu, with a troubled expression on his face. 'Why do you look so anxious?' Chuang Tzu asked. The ruler replied: 'I have studied the methods of the ancient rulers, and have tried to follow them. Yet I cannot avoid failure. That is why I look anxious.'

Chuang Tzu said: 'The elegant fox and the graceful snow leopard live in the mountain forests; that is where they are at peace. Since they both possess beautiful fur, they are constantly fearful of hunters. So they only go out at night to seek food, and they plan their trips with great care; during daylight they remain in their lairs. Nevertheless they are never entirely safe; they are always in danger of being caught in a trap or a net. So like you they always have an anxious expression. In their case their beautiful fur is the cause of anxiety; in your case it is the land that you rule. The fox and the leopard cannot rid themselves of their fur; but you are free to rid yourself of your kingdom. Your people would not suffer; on the contrary they would quickly learn to rule themselves.'

20

Never dying

Let me tell you the Way of never dying. There is a bird
dwelling near the eastern ocean that is completely helpless. It
has large wings, but these are too weak for flying. So it flips
and flops, and flops and flips – and can only fly with the
assistance of other birds. When the flock of birds is flying
from one place to another, none of the birds likes to be in
front, for fear of encountering danger; and none likes to be
at the back, for fear of being left behind. So all the birds like
to help the helpless bird, who is kept in the middle of the
flock. As a result the helpless bird is always safe.

20

Monkeys in thorn trees

Chuang Tzu dressed himself in an old robe made of coarse cloth covered in patches, and put on shoes held together with string; and he went to visit the king. The king asked: 'Why are you dressed like this?'

Chuang Tzu replied: 'This is poverty, but not distress. If I understood the Way, but was unable to follow it, that would be distress. But to wear an old robe and shoes held together with string – that is poverty, but not distress. Have you ever seen monkeys climbing? When they are among oak trees and plane trees, they leap freely from branch to branch, moving so fast that even the finest archer could not shoot them. But when they are among prickly thorn trees and mulberry trees, they move cautiously, looking anxiously from side to side. This is not because their limbs have become stiff, but because they are not in their natural environment, so they cannot use their skills. They are in distress.'

The king looked baffled. Chuang Tzu continued: 'You are like a monkey in a thorn tree, surrounded by rebellious ministers who are plotting to destroy you. Thus you are unable to use your skill as a ruler.' The king understood; he immediately removed the rebellious ministers, and replaced them with men who were loyal to him.

20

The only scholar

Chuang Tzu went to visit a certain king. The king said: 'There are many learned scholars in my kingdom, but few study your works.' Chuang Tzu replied: 'There are only a few learned scholars in your kingdom.' The king remonstrated: 'There are many men in my kingdom wearing scholarly dress. So how can you say there are only a few scholars?'

Chuang Tzu said: 'A man may wear the round cap and the square shoes of a scholar, but that does not mean he is truly learned. The test of true learning is whether a man follows the Way. I challenge you, therefore, to issue an order saying that anyone wearing the dress of a scholar, but not following the Way, will be executed.'

The king issued such an order. Within a few days only one man in the entire kingdom was wearing scholarly dress; he was extremely old and frail. The king summoned this man to his palace, and questioned him on all sorts of philosophical and political matters; the old man answered every question perfectly. Then the king asked the old man: 'Have you read the works of Chuang Tzu?' The old man replied: 'Those works are written on my soul.'

20

Finding the Way

An aristocrat asked Chuang Tzu: 'Where is the Way?' Chuang Tzu replied: 'It is everywhere.' The aristocrat persisted: 'Give me a specific example of where it is.' Chuang Tzu pointed to an ant on the ground, and said: 'It is in this ant.' 'Is that the lowest place where the Way is to be found?' the aristocrat asked. Chuang Tzu pointed to a blade of grass, and said: 'It is in that blade of grass.' 'Is that the lowest place where the Way is to be found?' the aristocrat asked. Chuang Tzu pointed to a stone on the ground, and said: 'It is in that stone.' 'Is that the lowest place where the Way is to be found?' the aristocrat asked. 'It is in shit and piss as well,' Chuang Tzu said.

The aristocrat looked shocked. Chuang Tzu said: 'Your questions miss the point. If you look for the Way in any specific thing, you will not find it. But if you look for the Way everywhere, then you will find it in every specific thing.'

22

Like a baby

Can you be a little baby? A baby cries all day, but its throat never becomes hoarse. A baby clenches its fists all day, but never gets cramp. The baby stares all day at everything going on around it, but is not affected by what it sees. A baby moves, yet does not know where it is going. A baby sits, but does not know where it is sitting.

If you can be like a baby, then you are following the Way.

23

Yin and yang going awry

When wood is rubbed against wood, flames spring up. When metal is put in fire, it melts and flows away. When yin and yang go awry, heaven and earth are thrown into chaos. We hear the crash and roll of thunder, and lightning flashes in the midst of rain, burning up huge trees. Men and women are apt to feel joy when there is no cause, and sorrow when there is no cause. They are apt to feel anxiety for no reason, and elation for no reason. Their minds are suspended between heaven and earth, and they are lost in bewilderment and delusion. Their emotions rub up against one another, lighting countless inner fires that upset their inner balance and harmony. Thus they cease to follow the Way.

26

The perch in a rut

Chou's family was very poor, so he went to borrow some grain from the local aristocrat. The aristocrat said: 'I shall soon be receiving rents from my land. So I should be glad to lend you three hundred pieces of silver. Will that be alright?'

Chou flushed with anger, and said: 'As I was coming here, I heard someone calling me. I turned round, and saw a perch in a carriage rut. I said to the perch: 'What are you doing here?' The perch replied: 'I was dropped here by a fisherman, who was taking me to the market. Could you pour a bucket of water into this rut, to keep me alive?' I replied: 'I shall change the course of the river, and send it in your direction. Will that be alright?' The perch flushed with anger, and said: 'I am out of my element. All I want is a bucket of water to keep me alive. But if you give me an answer like that, you may as well look for me in the dried fish store.'

26

The vast fish

A prince made an enormous fishhook, which he attached to a huge line. He attached an entire bullock onto the hook as bait. He then sat himself on top of a mountain overlooking the sea, and cast the line into the waves. For a whole year he caught nothing. At last a vast fish swallowed the bait, and dived down to the bottom of the sea, dragging down the bait and the hook with it. The prince held onto the line with all his strength. Then the vast fish rose up again and leapt out of the water; it flapped its fins, covering the mountain with spray. Finally the prince landed the fish. He cut it up into millions of pieces, and laid them out on the mountain to dry. Men and women from miles around came to the mountain, and the prince gave them as much dried fish as they could carry. Even when every person in the land had received a load of dried fish, there was still some left over.

Since that time people with meagre talents and a liking for tall stories have repeated this tale. Tall stories inspire people, and help them follow the Way.

26

According to nature

Chuang Tzu said to his disciples: 'If a man has an itch to travel, what can stop him? If someone does not wish to travel, what can force him? If someone wishes to conform, what can stop him? If someone wishes to be eccentric, what can prevent him? People should behave as their natures impel them to behave.

'Scholars are inclined to admire the past, and to despise the present. And if one were to compare the present age with the best age in the past, then one would be inclined to agree with scholarly opinion. Yet you cannot change the age in which you live. So let each age be as its nature impels it to be.'

26

Forgetting words

Chuang Tzu continued: 'The fish trap exists because of the fish; once you've caught the fish, you can forget the trap. The rabbit snare exists because of the rabbit; once you've caught the rabbit, you can forget the snare. Words exist because of their meaning; once you've grasped the meaning, you can forget the words. When I find people who have forgotten words, I can have a word with them.'

26

LIEH TZU

If Lieh Tzu existed as a distinct individual, he lived considerably earlier than Chuang Tzu, since Chuang Tzu refers to him as an ancient sage. But the book bearing his name was probably compiled a little after Chuang Tzu. It seems likely that later sages claimed to be spiritual heirs of Lieh Tzu, and as a result their deeds and sayings were attributed to him. So Lieh Tzu, as he appears in the book, is really a compilation of people.

The unborn and the unchanging

Lieh Tzu was living in a game reserve in the state of Cheng. For forty years no one regarded him as anybody special; the king, the nobles, and the high officials thought he was one of the common people. Nonetheless disciples gathered round him, recognizing that he was a man of great wisdom.

One summer Lieh Tzu decided to go on a journey alone. His disciples came to him, and asked him to teach them something before he went. Lieh Tzu said that he had nothing to teach. 'Then pass on something that your own teacher taught you,' they said. Lieh Tzu smiled, and said: 'He told me that there are the born and the unborn, the changing and unchanging. The unborn gives birth to the born, and the unchanging causes change in the changing. The born cannot escape birth, and the changing cannot escape changing; therefore birth and change are the norm.'

The disciples said: 'Tell us about the unborn and the unchanging.' Lieh Tzu said: 'The unborn is by our side, and yet alone; this is because it is boundless. The unchanging goes forth and returns; its going forth and returning is endless.'

The process of creation

Lieh Tzu continued: 'Just as the unborn gives birth to the born, so the shapeless gives shape to all objects. Yet from what were heaven and earth born? I answer: primal simplicity; primal start; primal beginning; and primal material. Primal simplicity preceded the appearance of breath. Primal start was the start of breath. Primal beginning was when breath began to assume shape. Primal material was when breath began to assume substance. When shape and substance were complete, things were still not separated from one another; there was confusion.

'Then shape and substance began to separate. One became two, then two became three, and so on. Yet even though things became separate, they did not lose their unity. This is the process of creation.'

1

The four changes

Lieh Tzu continued: 'From the beginning to the end people pass through four great changes: infancy, youth, old age, and death. In infancy their energies are concentrated and harmonized; that is why they are able to learn so much, and to withstand injury so easily. In youth they are in turmoil; anxieties and cares rise up within them, constantly threatening to overwhelm them — and they feel themselves constantly in competition with others. In old age these anxieties and cares diminish, and their bodies weaken; and they cease to compete with others. When they die, their energies are dispersed, and they can rest. The attainment of rest is the purpose of life.'

With these words Lieh Tzu departed from his disciples.

I

Four causes of joy

Lieh Tzu used to wear a rough fur coat with a rope round his waist. He wandered from place to place, strumming a lute and singing. One day someone asked him: 'Why are you always so joyful?'

He replied: 'I have four causes for joy. The first is that I am a human being, so I can enjoy all the pleasures of which the human body is capable. The second is that I am a man, so I can admire the beauties of women. The third is that I have now attained old age, so I have had a vast quantity of pleasure, compared with people who die young. And the fourth is that I am now ready to die, so have no fears or worries.

I

The happy old man

When Lin was nearly a hundred years old, he put on his fur coat, and went to pick grains dropped by the reapers. He sang as he walked through the fields. A disciple of Lieh Tzu, called Kung, saw him, and thought: 'That man possesses some special wisdom; I shall go and talk to him.' So Kung went over to Lin, and said: 'You are very old. Do you not feel any regret about your life?' Lin did not even look up, but carried on picking up grains and singing. Kung asked again whether he felt any regrets.

Lin then stopped, and said: 'What have I to regret? As a child I never learned how to behave. As a man I never strove for success. In my old age I live alone. And the time of my death is near.' Kung reframed his question: 'What happiness have you enjoyed, that you should sing so cheerfully?' Lin smiled, and replied: 'The causes of happiness are the same for everyone. Some people worry about being happy, and so they never attain happiness. I have never worried about being happy, so I have always been happy.'

Lin continued to pick up grains; and Kung went away satisfied.

I

The repose of death

Kung said one day to Lieh Tzu: 'I am weary of study; I want to find rest.' Lieh Tzu replied: 'There is no rest for the living.' 'Then shall I never find it?' Kung asked. Lieh Tzu replied: 'You shall. Think about your tomb; there you will find rest.' The disciple exclaimed: 'Death is great! The wise person looks forward to it, while the foolish person merely submits to it.'

Lieh Tzu said: 'Kung, you have grasped the truth. All people understood the sufferings of being alive, but few understand its joy. All people understand the weariness of growing old, but few understand its hope. All people understand the ugliness of death, but few understand its repose.'

I

Finding the true path

A disciple asked Lieh Tzu: 'Why do you value emptiness?' Lieh Tzu replied: 'In emptiness there is no valuing; that is why I value emptiness.'

The disciple was baffled. So Lieh Tzu continued: 'It is best to be still; it is best to be empty. In stillness and emptiness we find our true path. In taking and doing we lose our path.'

Lieh Tzu paused, and then added: 'Some people, when they go astray, start playing about with moral distinctions, in the hope of getting back on the right path. You can never find your path through morality.'

1

The collapse of heaven and earth

There was a man who was so worried that heaven and earth might collapse, and that he would have nowhere to go, that he forgot to eat and sleep. He had a friend who was greatly worried about him, and went to reassure him.

The friend said: 'Heaven is nothing but air; it cannot collapse.' The man said: 'If heaven is air, then the sun, the moon and the stars are liable to fall out of heaven, and hit people on earth.' The friend replied: 'The sun, the moon and the stars are simply lights inside air; they cannot fall down.' The man asked: 'What about the earth?.' The friend said: 'The earth is floating on air, so it too cannot collapse.' The man was reassured, and started eating and sleeping again.

Lieh Tzu was told about this conversation, and said: 'Of course, the man was right in his belief; heaven and earth will eventually collapse – all things are transient. But he was wrong in his response; there is no point in worrying about something over which we have no control.'

I

Possessing nothing

A man called Shun asked Lieh Tzu: 'Can I ever possess the Way?' Lieh Tzu replied: 'Your body is not your possession. So how can you possess the Way?' Shun said: 'If my body is not mine, whose it is?'

Lieh Tzu replied: 'Your body is the shape lent to you by heaven and earth. Your life is not your possession; it exists through the harmony of energies, and is lent for a time by heaven and earth. Your character and destiny are not your possessions; they are laid down for you by heaven and earth. Your children and grandchildren are not your possessions; you have cast them off from your body, as a snake sheds its skin. You travel through life without knowing where you are going; and you are fed, without knowing how food grows. So how can you ever possess anything?'

I

The right way of stealing

Kuo was very rich, and Hsiang was very poor. So Hsiang went to see Kuo, to ask how to become rich. Kuo said to him: 'I am rich because I am good at stealing. Within a year of being a thief I was comfortable; within two years I was affluent; and within three years I was a benefactor of the whole neighbourhood.'

So Hsiang decided to become a thief. He climbed over walls, broke into houses, and stole anything he could. But he was soon caught, and everything was taken from him. He thought Kuo had deceived him, and so he went to him to express his anger.

'In what way have you been stealing?' Kuo asked. Hsiang told him. Kuo said: 'Alas, you have not followed the true way of stealing. I rob heaven and earth. In the rainy season I steal rain, and irrigate my fields. I steal birds from the trees with my bow and arrow, and fish from the lakes with my fishing net. I steal silk from the silk worm to make clothes. In fact I spend every waking hour stealing, and that is how I have become rich. And heaven and earth never punish me for my thefts.'

So Hsiang took up stealing in the same way; and he too became a benefactor.

1

A dream of health

A king spent the first fifteen years of his reign indulging himself. He ate the finest foods, wore the sweetest perfumes, dressed in the softest silks, listened to the most skilled musicians, and surrounded himself with the most beautiful young women. As a consequence of this self-indulgence his flesh darkened and his senses dulled.

During the next fifteen years he worried about the government of his kingdom. He devoted all his time and intelligence to ruling the people. But his flesh continued to darken and his senses grew duller. Finally he exclaimed: 'I have cursed myself by caring for myself alone, and I have cursed myself by struggling to govern a vast empire!'

He now refused to concern himself with matters of policy, and he refused all bodily pleasures. He dismissed his servants, dispersed his musicians, and abandoned his palace; and for three months he lived in a hut in the palace courtyard. During this time he spoke to no one, and he fasted.

One day he fell asleep, and dreamt of a place where there are no leaders and teachers, but people live according to their natures. As a result they are healthy and happy, and no one dies young. They do not compete for wealth or privilege, they do not hold grudges, and they are never jealous of one another. When he awoke, he returned to his palace, and proclaimed himself king once again. But now he did not indulge himself, and nor did he attempt to rule his people. As a result both he and his people were healthy and happy.

2

The man on the mountain

The Ku mountain stands on an island where the Yellow River enters the sea. On this mountain lives a man of exceptional wisdom. He breathes the clear air that blows across the mountain, drinks the dew that falls on the mountain every night, and eats the wild fruits that grow on the mountain. He is a virgin, and has no desire for physical intimacy. He does not inspire awe in those who meet him; on the contrary, people feel calm and relaxed in his presence. He does not strive to be kind or generous, but is happy to listen or talk to anyone. He has no interest in wealth or fame.

In this man the yin and yang are in perfect harmony. Thus the sun and the moon are pleased to shine on him, the four seasons come and go on his mountain in due time, the climate is temperate, the wild fruits grow abundantly, and no plague ever comes to the mountain.

2

The indignant young man

A young man called Yi heard of Lieh Tzu, and came and lodged near his home. Ten times, when Lieh Tzu was not busy, Yi came to see him, and asked for the secrets of his wisdom. On each occasion Lieh Tzu refused to speak to him, and told him to go away. Yi felt more and more indignant; and finally, after several months he left.

Then a year later Yi returned. 'Why do you come and go and come back again?' Lieh Tzu asked him. Yi replied: 'A few months ago I asked you on ten occasions to tell me the secrets of your wisdom; and every time you refused to speak to me. I felt great resentment and rancour against you, but now those emotions have subsided. So I return.'

Lieh Tzu: 'Even though those emotions may have subsided, the propensity to feel them is as strong as ever. So you are no different now than when you left. If you come to see me tomorrow, I shall tell you about my experiences as a disciple of Shang. Then you will know whether you truly wish to be a disciple of mine.'

2

Lieh Tzu as a disciple

Yi returned to Lieh Tzu the next day, and Lieh Tzu told him about his experiences as a disciple of Shang: 'For three years Shang never even glanced at me. At the end of that time my mind no longer dared to think about right and wrong; and my mouth no longer dared to speak of benefit and harm. Then Shang spoke to me once; I was so astounded, that I did not listen to what he said. A further five years passed; and at the end of that time my mind was again thinking about right and wrong, and my mouth was speaking about benefit and harm. Then Shang turned to me, and for the first time his face relaxed in a smile. A further seven years passed. At the end of that time I was allowing my mind to think whatever it wanted, without distinguishing between right and wrong; and I was allowing my mouth to say whatever it wanted, without distinguishing between benefit and harm.

'Then Shang invited me to sit next to him on his mat. A further nine years passed. At the end of that time I no longer regarded Shang as my teacher; I now regarded him as a friend. My eyes had become like my ears, my ears like my nose, and my nose like my mouth; all my senses had become unified. My mind was in harmony, my body relaxed, and I was no longer concerned where I was. So I left Shang and returned home.'

Lieh Tzu stared intently at Yi, and said: 'You come to be my disciple, and within a few months are overwhelmed with rancour and resentment. Do you seriously hope to enter the realm of stillness and inaction?' Yi remained with Lieh Tzu for many years; but he never spoke again.

Walking under water

A disciple said to Lieh Tzu: 'It is said that wise people can walk under water, and not drown; and tread on fire, and not burn. How do they achieve this?'

Lieh Tzu replied: 'It has nothing to do with skill and courage. Whatever has shape and colour, is an object. How can one object put a distance between itself and other objects? How can it become superior to other objects? It is merely shape and colour. But wise people can understand that which has no shape; they know that all shapes are created from it. They can understand that which has no colour; they know that all colours are created from it. For this reason nothing can stop wise people. Their minds are at peace and their energies are in harmony. If you can be like this, you will be able to walk under water without drowning, and tread on fire without burning.'

2

The art of archery

A disciple called Po asked Lieh Tzu to demonstrate the art of archery. Lieh Tzu put a bowl of water on his left forearm. Then he took a bow, placed an arrow within it, drew it to the full, and shot the arrow. The arrow hit the target, and the water in the bowl remained absolutely still. Lieh Tzu shot several more arrows; and the water remained still.

Po then asked Lieh Tzu to climb up a high mountain, put one foot over a cliff, and again show the art of archery. So together they climbed up a high mountain, carrying a bow, several arrows, and a bowl of water. At the top Leih Tzu went to the edge of a cliff, and put one foot over the edge. Then he put the bowl of water on his left forearm, took the bow, placed an arrow within it, drew it to the full, and shot the arrow. The arrow hit the target, and the water in the bowl remained absolutely still. Lieh Tzu shot several more arrows; and the water remained still.

In the meantime, as he watched Lieh Tzu shooting the arrows with one foot over the edge of the cliff, Po was sweating with fear; and when Lieh Tzu had finished shooting, Po fainted. After Po had recovered, the two men returned home. As they climbed down the mountain, Lieh Tzu said to Po: 'Now you have learnt that anxiety and fear are in the mind, not in the situation.'

2

The old peasant's powers

There was once a chief minister called Hua, who was feared by the whole country. He employed strong and intelligent officials and soldiers, and he encouraged them to bully everyone they encountered. If an official or soldier proved particularly good at instilling fear in people, Hua rewarded him richly.

An old peasant called Kai decided to visit Hua's mansion. When he arrived, Hua's officials and soldiers noticed his weather-beaten face and emaciated body, and decided to humiliate him; they called him rude names, and hit him with sticks. Kai showed no anger or fear, and eventually they grew tired of their sport.

Hua came out of his mansion. As a joke he pointed to the roof of his mansion, and said: 'If anyone can jump off my roof, I shall reward that person with a hundred pieces of gold.' Kai climbed up onto the roof, and jumped off. He fell slowly through the air like a feather, and landed safely. Hua rewarded him.

Hua then threw a diamond ring into the river, and challenged Kai to fetch it out. Kai dived into the water; and several minutes later he emerged, with the ring in his hand. Hua gave him the ring.

A few days later Hua's storehouse caught fire. Hua begged Kai to go into the flames, and rescue his fine brocades. Kai walked calmly into the burning storehouse, and one by one took out the brocades.

2

Ruling through love

Hua, his officials and soldiers were now convinced that Kai possessed supernatural powers; and instead of trying to frighten him, they were themselves frightened that he might use his powers against them.

So Hua asked Kai: 'How are you able to jump off a high roof, swim under water for many minutes, and walk into a burning building, without getting hurt?' Kai replied: 'I follow the Way. So there is perfect harmony within my mind and soul; my thoughts and emotions are at peace. Anyone with inner harmony could do these things.' Hua asked: 'How could I acquire inner harmony?'

Kai smiled, and said: 'What is your motive for wanting inner harmony? If your motive is to possess supernatural powers, then you will never acquire it. But if you want inner harmony for its own sake, and are indifferent to those powers, then you can acquire it.'

Hua knew that his motive was wrong; so he asked Kai how he could purify his motive. Kai replied: 'If you no longer wish to instil fear in people, then you will cease to be interested in possessing supernatural powers.' So from that moment onwards Hua ceased to rule people through fear, and instead ruled them through love. And gradually he too learnt how to jump off a high roof, swim under water for many minutes, and walk into a burning building, without getting hurt.

2

Escape from a fire

Lieh Tzu was staying alone in a house one night. During the night a terrible thunderstorm arose, and lightning struck the house. As flames rose high in the sky, the neighbours rushed to the house; but the heat was so intense that no one dared enter. Then to their astonishment Lieh Tzu walked calmly out of the fire and into the street. His clothes were badly scorched, but his skin was unhurt.

'How have you survived, and how have you escaped injury?' the people asked. Lieh Tzu smiled: 'I know that the moment of my death is already determined; so nothing can frighten me. And I am utterly indifferent as to whether I live or whether I die; so nothing can harm me.'

2

The man and the seagulls

There was a man living by the seashore who loved seagulls. Every morning he went down to the beach, and the seagulls flew down to him from their nests in the cliffs. They gathered round him, shrieking at the tops of their voices; and he too shrieked with pleasure. He danced across the beach, and they danced with him.

One day his father said to him: 'I too would like to dance with seagulls. Tomorrow morning you must catch some seagulls, and bring them to me.' The man felt very sad; he believed that seagulls should be free, so he hated the idea of catching any of them. Nonetheless he had a duty to obey his father.

So the next morning he went to the beach, with the intention of catching some seagulls, and taking them to his father. But none of the seagulls flew down; they remained firmly in their nests.

2

The respectful innkeepers

Lieh Tzu was on his way to the capital city; but when he had covered half the journey, he turned back. As he was walking along the road, he met an old friend.

'Why have you turned back?' the friend asked. 'I was alarmed by something,' Lieh Tzu replied. 'What alarmed you?' the friend asked. Lieh Tzu replied: 'I stopped to eat at ten inns; and at each one the innkeeper served me first, before serving any of the other travellers.' 'Why should that alarm you?' the friend asked.

Lieh Tzu replied: 'It is a sign I am not following the Way. Deep within me I must be wanting power and status; and this conveys itself to people I meet – so, out of kindness to me, they treat me with special respect. That is why the innkeepers served me first. If I had continued my journey to the capital city, the king himself might have treated me with special respect, and offered me some high office; and out of my desire for power and status, I should have accepted his offer.'

'So what will you do now?' the friend asked. Lieh Tzu replied: 'I shall return home, and I shall teach myself once again to follow the Way.'

2

Acquiring humility

A young nobleman called Yang decided to visit Lieh Tzu, in order to learn the Way. As he travelled to Lieh Tzu's house, people knew from his bearing that he was a nobleman. So at every inn the innkeeper served him first, the innkeeper's wife brought him warm water to wash his hands and face, and the other guests bowed to him.

Yang spent a year with Lieh Tzu; and by the end he was following the Way. So he decided to return home. To his surprise the innkeepers no longer served him first, their wives did not bring him water, and the other guests did not bow to him. As he reflected on this, he was overjoyed. He said to himself: 'I must have acquired humility – so truly I am following the Way.'

2

The two mistresses

Lieh Tzu was travelling through a certain area, and spent the night at an inn. The innkeeper had two mistresses, one beautiful and the other ugly. Lieh Tzu observed that the innkeeper treated the ugly one with great tenderness and respect, whereas he neglected the beautiful one.

Lieh Tzu asked the innkeeper the reason for this. The innkeeper replied: 'The beautiful woman is so vain and self-satisfied that she does not notice how I treat her. The ugly woman is so self-effacing and humble that she responds to my tenderness with gratitude – and this pleases me.'

Lieh Tzu later related this story to his disciples, and concluded: 'If a woman's ugliness can evoke a man's love, then you should learn to regard every curse as a blessing.'

2

Strength and weakness

Lieh Tzu said to his disciples: 'Some people are strong, and some are weak. Strong people often enjoy oppressing the weak; so when a strong man meets someone even stronger than himself, he is frightened that he himself will be oppressed. The weak, by contrast, learn guile; they find ways of giving the impression of being oppressed, while in fact preserving their freedom. Thus we may say that while the strong are stronger than the weak, the weak are stronger than the strong.

'But what do we mean by strength and weakness? The strong may try to control the weak; but if they cannot control their own minds and souls, their strength is an illusion. In order to learn guile, the weak must find ways of controlling their minds and souls; and by this means they become stronger than the strong.'

2

Softness and hardness

Lieh Tzu said to his disciples: 'If your aim is to be hard, you must learn to be soft. If your aim is to be strong, you must learn to be weak. As softness accumulates, it gradually becomes hard; as weakness accumulates, it gradually becomes strong. If you watch them accumulate, you will learn the nature of both blessings and curses. The strong may conquer those weaker than themselves; but when two strong people meet one another, they are liable to injure and even destroy one another. When the weak learn to outwit those stronger than themselves, their strength is beyond measure.

'If a weapon is hard and strong, it will snap in battle. If a tree is hard and strong, it will break in the wind. Softness and weakness bring life; hardness and strength bring death.'

2

Appearance and intelligence

Lieh Tzu said: 'A living being may be as wise and intelligent as a human being, but not look like a human being. Foolish people only like the company of other humans, who look like themselves. Wise people like the company of all intelligent living beings, regardless of their appearance. A living being who walks on two legs, and has hair only on the head, is called a human; but that appearance signifies nothing about intelligence. A living being with wings is called a bird, and a living being with horns is called an animal; but their appearance signifies nothing about intelligence.

'I am as willing to teach animals and birds as to teach humans. My only concern is that my disciples should possess sufficient intelligence to understand me.'

2

Training cocks

A man called Chi was employed by the king to train cocks for fighting. One day a merchant came to the king, and offered to sell him cocks that were twice as large as any the king had seen before. The king paid a high price for these large cocks, and gave them to Chi for training.

After ten days the king came to Chi, and asked: 'Are the cocks ready to fight yet?' Chi replied: 'No. At present they just strut around, showing off their size and strength.'

After another ten days the king came to Chi, and again asked: 'Are the cocks ready to fight yet?' Chi replied: 'No. At present they enjoy showing aggression, even to their own shadows.'

After another ten days the king came to Chi, and again asked: 'Are the cocks ready to fight yet?' Chi replied: 'Yes. They feel no need to show off, and they never show aggression. From a distance they look like statues carved in wood. Their virtue is complete. So when another cock sees them, it will be terrified, and will run away.'

2

The Way of love

Lieh Tzu went to visit the king, and the king said to him: 'I take no pleasure in people who preach morality. What have you to teach me?' Lieh Tzu replied: 'Suppose that I could teach you a Way, so that, if anyone tried to stab you, then you would be able to deflect the knife. Would you be interested?' The king replied: 'Yes, certainly I should be interested.'

Lieh Tzu then said: 'Suppose that I could teach you a Way, so that you instilled great fear in people; thus no one would dare to attack you. Would you be interested?' The king replied: 'Yes, certainly I should be interested.'

Lieh Tzu then said: 'Suppose that I could teach you a Way, so that you instilled great love in people; thus no one would want to attack you, and everyone would want to serve you. Would you be interested?' The king replied: 'Yes, certainly I should be interested.'

Lieh Tzu: 'This Way requires you to give up all attempts to rule your people, and instead let them rule themselves. The people will then flourish and prosper, and they will hold you responsible for their happiness. Thus they will love you beyond measure, and they will be eager to serve you in any way you wish.'

The king was at a loss for an answer.

2

Physical blindness and deafness

A wise man called Wen, who possessed magical powers, came to visit the king. Wen could walk under water without drowning, tread on fire without burning, pierce metal and stone with his fingers, and throw himself off high buildings without injury.

The king was so impressed by these feats that he worshipped Wen as if he were divine. He gave Wen the most luxurious chamber in the palace in which to live, provided him with the most beautiful young women in the kingdom as servants, and supplied him with the most delicious food that the palace kitchens could prepare. But Wen pretended to be discontent with all this. So the king built Wen his own palace, which was even bigger than his own.

Wen now had a firm hold on the king's mind. So one day he went to see the king, and ordered him to close his eyes. Wen now took the king on a mental journey. Led by Wen the king flew upwards through the sky, until they reached a place of such brightness that the king was blinded. Then a humming noise began, that became so loud that the king was deafened. The king now shook with fear. Wen kicked the king in the back, and the king fell downwards through the sky like a metoer; he landed back in his palace.

3

Mental sight and hearing

The king remained deaf and blind for several years. His inability to see or hear his people prevented him from exercising any authority. As a result his people flourished and prospered. Finally the king's sight and hearing returned. The first person he saw and heard was Wen, the wise man with magical powers.

Wen said to him: 'Several years ago I took you on a mental journey, which caused you to become physically blind and deaf. Now I am going to take you on a physical journey, which will give you mental sight and hearing.' Wen led the king round his kingdom. They visited every town and village, and spoke to all the people. The people greeted the king with joy, and thanked him for ruling the kingdom with such wisdom. The king was overjoyed at their happiness.

When the king and Wen had completed their journey, they both turned their palaces into hospitals for the old and sick; and they each went to live in an ordinary house in an ordinary neighbourhood.

3

Magical powers

A young man called Leo heard of Wen's magical powers, and went to see him. 'I should like to acquire the same magical powers as you possess,' Leo said. Wen bowed to Leo, indicating that he would be willing to accept him as a disciple.

For three years Wen did not speak to Leo. Finally in frustration Leo begged him: 'Please say something to me, or else I shall leave.' Wen smiled and said: 'Look around you. The world is full of plants and trees, animals and birds. Each living being has been shaped by yin and yang; and when yin and yang depart from a living being, that being dies. None of us can understand this continuous process of creation and destruction; we simply observe it with wonder. Now consider my magical powers. I can walk under water without drowning, tread on fire without burning, pierce metal and stone with my fingers, and throw myself off high buildings without injury. These may seem impressive; but they are trivial compared with the creation and destruction of a single living being.'

Leo understood these words, and so became wise. And having become wise, he also acquired the same magical powers that Wen possessed; but he now had no interest in those powers.

3

Dreaming and waking

A man came to see Lieh Tzu, and asked him to explain the mystery of dreaming. Lieh Tzu replied: 'Dreams reflect the state of yin and yang within you. When yin is strong, you dream of walking through deep waters, and you feel cold. When yang is strong, you dream of walking through blazing fire, and you feel hot. When yin and yang are both strong, you dream of killing or sparing other living beings.'

The man said: 'This does not explain the whole range of dreams.' Lieh Tzu continued: 'When you overeat, you dream of receiving presents; when you eat too little, you dream of giving presents. When you suffer from giddiness, you dream of floating in the air; when you have a sinking feeling, you dream of drowning. When you go to sleep in your belt, you dream of snakes; when a bird pecks your hair, you dream of flying. When you fall asleep after drinking wine, your dreams are anxious; when you fall asleep after singing and dancing, your dreams are tearful.'

The young man said: 'Tell me about the differences between waking experiences and dreaming experiences.' Lieh Tzu replied: 'Waking experiences are determined by what the body encounters; dreams are determined by what the spirit encounters.'

3

Three countries

Lieh Tzu said to his disciples: 'In the far south of the earth there is a country where yin and yang do not meet; thus there is no distinction between cold and heat. The sun and the moon do not shine; so there is no distinction between day and night. Its people do not eat or wear clothes, and they spend most of their time asleep. They regard their dreams as real, and their waking experiences as unreal.

'In the middle of the earth there is a country where yin and yang are in perfect proportion; so there is distinction between cold and heat. The sun and the moon both shine; so there is alternation between day and night. Some if its people are wise, and some are foolish. There are many kinds of skills and abilities; there are rulers and officials to oversee the use of these skills and abilities; and there are customs and laws to preserve order. The people wake and sleep in succession. They regard their waking experiences as real, and their dreams as unreal.

'In the north of the earth there is a country where yin and yang are excessively strong. The climate is unbearably hot, because the sun and the moon shine too brightly. The soil is too parched to produce crops, so the people live on wild herbs and roots. The hot climate and poor diet make the people harsh and fierce, so the strong oppress the weak. They are always awake and never sleep.'

3

Hope and dread

A man called Chou had a vast estate. He compelled his servants to work hard from dawn to dusk each day, and allowed them no rest. There was a servant called Fu who was weak and frail; and Chou drove him even harder than the rest.

One day Fu came to visit Lieh Tzu, and complained about Chou's harsh regime. Lieh Tzu said to Fu: 'Just before you fall asleep at night, imagine yourself living a life of ease; then in your dreams you will experience this life.' Fu did as Lieh Tzu instructed. As a result his nights were pleasant; and even during the day he felt better, because his soul was filled with hope – the hope that one day his dreams would be realized.

Late one night Lieh Tzu went to visit Chou. Lieh Tzu said: 'Imagine yourself as one of your own servants – such as Fu.' Lieh Tzu then left. Shortly afterwards Chou fell asleep, and dreamt that he was Fu. The thought of being Fu then stuck in his mind. So every night he continued to dream of being Fu; and during the day he dreaded that his dream might be realized.

Lieh Tzu then invited both men to his house, and asked: 'Which of you is better off: Fu, whose nights are pleasant, and whose days are full of hope; or Chou whose nights are miserable, and whose days are full of dread?' Chou knew at once the answer to that question; and from that moment he treated Fu and all his servants with kindness and compassion.

3

The deer in a ditch

A woodcutter called Cheng went into the forest each day to collect firewood. One day he encountered a deer. The deer was so frightened that it did not move. Cheng struck it, and killed it. Since he was unable to carry both firewood and the deer, he decided to bury the deer in a ditch, with the intention of returning later to collect it.

The next day Cheng went back to the forest, but could not find the ditch where he had buried the deer. Eventually he concluded that he must have dreamt the whole incident. That evening he mentioned this in his village. A few days later a neighbour called Yan went to the forest in order to search for the dead deer; and after several hours looking in ditches, he found it. He brought it home, cut it in pieces, and sold the pieces to the people of the village.

When Cheng realized that Yan had found his deer and sold it, he was furious. He went to Yan, and said: 'I killed that deer; so I should have the money which you have received for its meat.' But Yan refused to hand him the money. So they both went to Lieh Tzu, and asked him to pass judgement.

3

Reality and dreaming

After he had heard the full story, Lieh Tzu said to Cheng: 'If you really did catch the deer, you were wrong to think that you dreamt of catching it. If you really dreamt that you caught the deer, you are wrong now to claim the money for it. It seems that you are unable to distinguish between dreaming and waking.'

Then he said to Yan: 'When you heard Cheng tell the story of the deer, you realized that he was confused about waking and dreaming; so you took advantage of his confusion by going in search of the deer. It seems that you distinguish too clearly between waking and dreaming.'

Lieh Tzu then passed judgement: 'Since Cheng cannot distinguish between waking and dreaming, he would not know whether the money was real or not. Since Yan distinguishes too clearly between waking and dreaming, he regards money as more important than it is. Therefore the money must be handed to me, and I shall give it to the poor.'

Yan handed Lieh Tzu the money, and he gave it to the poor. Cheng and Yan now became close friends. Yan helped Cheng to distinguish between waking and dreaming; and Cheng helped Yan to realize that reality and dreaming are equally important.

3

Response to memory

A middle-aged man called Li lost his memory. By evening he had forgotten what had occurred in the morning; and by morning he had forgotten what had occurred the previous evening. In the street he forgot to walk, and at home he forgot to sit down. He himself was quite content, but his family were deeply worried.

His family sent messengers far and wide, to seek a doctor who could cure him. A last they found a doctor who specialized in restoring lost memories. The doctor came to Li, and treated him; and after a few weeks Li's memory returned. Li's contentment now changed to anger and resentment. Each evening, as he remembered what had occurred to him in the morning, he was convinced that he had been badly treated. And each morning, as he recalled what had happened the previous evening, he believed that the bad treatment had continued. Thus he frequently hit his wife and children with sticks.

In their distress his family sent messengers far and wide, to seek someone who could restore Li's contentment. Eventually they found Lieh Tzu. Lieh Tzu said to Li: 'The past is over. All that remains is your memory of it. So why be angry with other people about something that is inside your own head?' This question confounded Li; and he was never angry again.

3

Reverse perception

Pang had a son who was extremely intelligent; but as he grew up, he developed a strange abnormality. When he heard singing, he thought it was weeping; when he saw white, he thought it was black; when he smelt perfume, he was repelled; when he tasted sweet foods, he found them bitter; when he saw someone doing something wicked, he thought the action right. Thus in his mind he turned everything upside down.

The father asked Lieh Tzu to treat him. Lieh Tzu talked with the child at length, and then said to the father: 'You believe that your son has a sickness of the mind. Yet it is quite possible that his perceptions are correct, and other people's perceptions are incorrect. If the whole world perceived things as your son does, then singing would be regarded as weeping, white would be seen as black, perfume would be regarded as repulsive, sweet foods would be rejected as bitter, and morality standards would be reversed. So your son may be well, and the rest of us may be sick.'

3

A joke on an old man

An old man had been born in the town of Yen; but as a young man he had moved to the province of Chu, where he had remained. His memories of his native land had become blurred with the passing of years. So he decided to return there, to see it once more before he died; and a group of younger companions offered to accompany him.

As they were passing through a town called Chin, his companions decided to play a joke on him. They declared: 'We have arrived! This is your native town of Yen.' The old man was filled with joy. They took him to a shrine, and said: 'This is where you worshipped as a small boy.' The old man breathed a deep sigh, and said a prayer. They took him to an old cottage, and said: 'This is where you were born, and where you lived with your parents.' Tears welled up in the old man's eyes. Finally they took him to a mound, and said: 'This is where your father is buried.' The old man now wept aloud.

His companions roared with laughter, and told him of their joke. The old man was upset. But he composed himself, and they continued to Yen. When the old man saw the real shrine, his parents' actual cottage, and his father's genuine tomb, he was hardly moved at all.

As he was returning to Chu, the old man met Lieh Tzu. He told him of the joke that his companions had played, and his lack of emotion when he finally reached his native town. Lieh Tzu concluded: 'Your journey has not been wasted. At last you have learnt that emotions are not a reliable guide to the truth.'

The words of a lute

Lieh Tzu became sad because the king was ruling the country incompetently. He sat alone on his bed, staring gloomily out of the window.

One of his disciples, called Yen, decided to sit outside the window and play the lute, in the hope of lifting the spirits of his master. As soon as he heard the lute, Lieh Tzu rose up, leaned out of the window, and exclaimed: 'How dare you play music in my ear! The cheerful sound of your lute irritates me beyond measure.' Yen replied: 'You have told your disciples many times to accept their destiny without complaint, and so be free of cares. Your destiny is to live under an incompetent king.'

Lieh Tzu said nothing, and returned to his bed. Yen continued to play his lute. The following day Lieh Tzu came out of his house, with a serene smile on his face. He embraced Yen, and said: 'Thank you. You have taught me to listen to myself. And when I listen to myself, I can listen to your music with pleasure.'

4

Easing the king's mind

The king felt anxious and confused, and decided that he wanted to consult a man of wisdom, in order to ease his mind. So he sent one of his officials to find the wisest man in the land. The official went in one direction, and found a wise man who was able to discard his mind, and live only as a body. He went in another direction, and found a wise man who was able to look with his ears and listen with his eyes. Then going in a third direction he found Lieh Tzu.

'Are you able to discard your mind?' the official asked. 'No,' Lieh Tzu replied. 'Are you able to look with your ears and listen with your eyes?' the official asked. 'No,' Lieh Tzu replied. 'What can you do?' the official asked. Lieh Tzu replied: 'I can look and listen without using eyes and ears.'

The official decided that Lieh Tzu was the wisest man in the land, and invited him to visit the king. The king asked Lieh Tzu: 'How are you able to look and listen without eyes and ears?' Lieh Tzu replied: 'My body is in harmony with my mind; my mind is in harmony with my energies; my energies are in harmony with my soul; and my soul is in harmony with nothing. Thus I can discern the faintest sound and the tiniest movement, even if they occur on the furthest edge of the world.'

'May I ask your advice whenever I need it?' the king asked. 'Yes,' Lieh Tzu replied. This assurance eased the king's mind – even though he never actually sought Lieh Tzu's advice.

4

True wisdom

A wealthy merchant asked Lieh Tzu: 'If a man studied widely and remembered much, would you call him wise?' 'No,' replied Lieh Tzu.

'If a man possessed great courage, would you call him wise?' the merchant asked. 'No,' Lieh Tzu replied.

'If a man always abided by the highest standards of morality, would you call him wise?' the merchant asked. 'No,' Lieh Tzu replied.

'If a man were good at adapting himself to the times and circumstances in which he found himself, would you call him wise?' the merchant asked. 'No,' Lieh Tzu replied.

'So who would you call wise?' the merchant asked. Lieh Tzu replied: 'There is a ruler in the west who is wise. He does not govern, yet there is no disorder. He does not speak, yet people trust him. He tries not to change things, yet his influence prevails. He is so wise that none of his people give him a name.'

4

The balance of virtues

Another wealthy merchant asked Lieh Tzu: 'What sort of man is your disciple Yen?' Lieh Tzu replied: 'For kindness he is better than I am.'

'What sort of man is your disciple Kung?' Lieh Tzu replied: 'For eloquence he is better than I am.'

'What sort of man is your disciple Lu?' Lieh Tzu replied: 'For courage he is better than I am.'

'What sort of man is your disciple Chang?' Lieh Tzu replied: 'For dignity he is better than I am.'

The merchant was perplexed. He asked: 'If each of these is superior to you in some virtue, why are they your disciples. Surely they should be the masters, and you the disciple.'

Lieh Tzu smiled and said: 'They are my disciples because they asked to be. And they made this request because they know that wisdom does not consist in excelling in some particular virtue.' 'In what does wisdom consist?' the merchant asked. Lieh Tzu replied: 'It consists in finding the perfect balance of virtues.'

4

The pompous neighbour

Lieh Tzu's nearest neighbour was a man called Nan. For forty years the two men never spoke; even when they passed in the street, their eyes never met.

One day a disciple of Lieh Tzu said to him: 'Surely it is wrong that you have never spoken to your nearest neighbour. I think that you should lead your disciples to his house, and pay your respects to him.' Lieh Tzu nodded, but said nothing. Later that day his disciples formed a line; and he led them to Nan's house.

When they arrived, Nan came out to see them. He was fat, and dressed in brightly coloured robes. He immediately began to hector Lieh Tzu and his disciples, telling them what to believe and how to behave. He spoke for a long time in this fashion, never stopping to ask for a reply. Eventually, while Nan was still talking, Lieh Tzu led his disciples away.

When they arrived back at Lieh Tzu's home, he said: 'If a man knows little, he says much. If a man is foolish, he asserts his wisdom.'

4

Outward and inward travel

A disciple said to Lieh Tzu: 'I have been told that, when you were young, you liked to travel. But now you rarely go far from your house. What has caused this change in your habits?'

Lieh Tzu replied: 'Initially I travelled to amuse myself; I enjoyed seeing different places and people. Then I travelled to see how places and people change; I went to places that I had visited before, and observed how places and people alter with the passage of time. Finally it occurred to me that I should be concerned with only one kind of change: the change within my own soul. So I gave up outward travel, and took up inward travel instead.'

4

Sick with wisdom

One of the king's officials came to Lieh Tzu, and said: 'I am seriously ill.' Lieh Tzu said: 'Describe your symptoms to me.' The official said: 'I have ceased to care whether people praise me or revile me. I take no pleasure in success, and feel no anxiety about failure. I no longer desire wealth, and I no longer dread poverty. I am happy to live, and am equally happy to die.'

Lieh Tzu exclaimed: 'You have discovered wisdom, and yet regard it as a disease!' The official said: 'As an official of the king I am expected to be ambitious for power, status and wealth. The king only trusts ambitious people, because he can control them by offering or withholding power, status and wealth. So as a consequence of my condition, the king no longer trusts me.'

Lieh Tzu said: 'Then you must resign from your position, and give up the power, status and wealth that goes with it.' When the official heard these words, the desire for power, status and wealth was reawakened in him. 'You have cured me!' he declared. He returned to the king, and told him that he was again ambitious; and the king again trusted him.

4

From and to nowhere

Lieh Tzu gathered his disciples, and said: 'When you are born, you come from nowhere; that is the Way. When you live according to your nature, that is the Way. When you die, you go nowhere; that is the Way.

'Since you come from nowhere, you depend on nothing; to remain dependent on nothing is the Way. Since you go nowhere, you accumulate nothing; to remain poor is the Way.

'When people die, their relatives usually weep. But if a person has followed the Way, the relatives should sing.'

4

The limit

Lieh Tzu continued: 'When the eye can discern the tip of a hair, it is about to go blind. When an ear can discern the wings of a gnat, it is about to go deaf. When the tongue can discern the difference between the waters of one river and another, it is about to lose its sense of taste. When the nose can discern the difference between the odour of scorching linen and scorching silk, it is about to lose its sense of smell. When the body takes special delight in sprinting, the limbs are about to stiffen. And when the mind distinguishes most sharply between right and wrong, it is about to go astray.

'So do not push yourself to the limit.'

4

Other people's minds

A man called Kung became famous for his strength. The king heard about him, and summoned him to his palace.

When the king saw Kung, he was astonished how puny he looked. He beckoned Kung to come up to him, and he put his hand on Kung's arms and legs. Then he exclaimed: 'You have barely a muscle on your body. You must be the weakest person in the land, not the strongest.'

Kung replied: 'My strength lies in other people's heads.' The king was perplexed, and demanded that Kung explain himself. Kung replied: 'My explanation lies in the very fact that you summoned me to your palace.' The king was even more perplexed, and demanded a fuller explanation.

Kung said: 'The truth is that I like to sit at home, and to study ancient books. But in the past I was constantly disturbed by big, strong lads, who came to my home, dragged me outside, and beat me. So one day I decided to go and visit Lieh Tzu, and ask his advice. He invited me to stay with him for a few months. During this time he sent a message back to my town, saying that I was being trained as a wrestler, and was now immensely strong. Then one night, when the moon was not shining, Lieh Tzu instructed me to return home. Since that time I have never gone out, except on dark, moonless nights; as a result no one has ever seen me. But everyone is terrified of me – so I can study ancient books in peace.'

4

Simple skills

A man called Lung came to the king, and said: 'I can teach you to shoot ten arrows, so that the point of each arrow hits the notch of the one in front. And I can teach you to shoot an arrow at someone's eye so that it causes no injury.' The king was astonished, and asked Lung to teach him these two skills. Lung then added: 'I shall only teach them to you, if you first give me a fine mansion in which to live.'

The king gave Lung a fine mansion, and Lung set about teaching him the two skills. The first skill proved simple: the king merely had to shoot one arrow after another without changing his stance. The second was even simpler: he had to measure how far an arrow travelled before losing its power, and then shoot from that distance. Within a morning the king had acquired both skills, and was immensely pleased with himself. He thanked Lung profusely.

Lieh Tzu heard what had happened, and sent a message to the king: 'When they sow and reap their crops, ordinary peasants demonstrate greater skills than Lung possesses. I trust you will be even more generous with the peasants in your land than you have been with Lung.' When he received this message, the king knew that he had been cheated by Lung; but he could not take back Lung's mansion without admitting his own folly. So he redeemed his error by doing as Lieh Tzu advised – he gave away almost all his wealth to the common people.

4

Good rule

When Yao had been king for fifty years, he wondered whether the people wished him to continue. So he asked his ministers: 'Are the people happy with my rule?' But his ministers did not know. He asked the distinguished visitors who came to his court: 'Are the people happy with my rule?' But the visitors did not know.

He decided he must find out for himself whether the people were happy. He disguised himself as a humble peasant, and walked from town to town throughout the land. Everywhere he went he asked people: 'Are you happy?' And invariably they said: 'Yes.' Then he asked: 'What makes you happy?' And they replied: 'We are happy because we follow the Way – and the king does not interfere.'

The king returned to his palace, and said to his ministers: 'The people are happy with my rule because I do nothing. Therefore I must find a successor who will also do nothing.' He summoned a man called Shun, who had been a disciple of Lieh Tzu, and asked him to become king. Shun accepted, and Yao abdicated.

4

Like water, a mirror and a gorge

Lieh Tzu summoned his disciples, and said to them: 'If your soul is not rigid, but is constantly flexible, it will be able to move like water, be still like a mirror, and echo like a deep gorge.

'Sometimes people abandon the Way; but the Way abandons no one. In order to follow the Way, you should not use your eyes or ears; you should not exert yourself, nor should you think. If you try to follow the Way by using your eyes and ears, by exerting yourself, or by thinking rationally, you will miss it.

'Observe the Way in front of you, and suddenly it is behind you. Think about the Way, and suddenly you have forgotten all about it. Strive to follow the Way, and you will stumble. Presence of mind cannot bring the Way nearer, and absence of mind does not make it more distant. It can be heard only through deafness, and seen only through blindness.

'To know without passion is the means of recognizing the Way. To act without exertion is the means of following the Way.'

4

Starting and ending

A wealthy merchant asked Lieh Tzu: 'Have there always been things?' Lieh Tzu replied: 'If once there were no things, how is it that there are things now? How would you feel if people of the future, looking back at the present time, were to say that there were no things then?'

The merchant continued: 'Does each individual thing only exist in the present?' Lieh Tzu replied: 'The ending and starting of things have no limit. The start of one thing is the end of another. The end of one thing is the start of another. Who knows which came first?'

The merchant continued: 'Does each individual thing have limited duration?' Lieh Tzu smiled, and said: 'I do not know.'

The house and the mountain

A man called Tai lived near a very high mountain. When he reached the age of ninety, he began to feel upset that the mountain blocked the way to his house, so visitors had to walk round the mountain in order to reach him. So he called his family together, and said: 'I propose that we dig a valley straight through the mountain.' Every member of the family agreed, except his wife who said to him: 'You are too weak to dig. Besides, where will you put the earth and stones?' Tai replied: 'I am not too weak. And we shall throw the earth and stones down the side of the mountain.'

The next day Tai, accompanied by his sons and grandsons, began to dig. It was summer, and Tai sweated profusely as he worked. Summer turned to winter, and Tai shivered as he worked. But despite their efforts, they made hardly any impression on the mountain.

Then one day Lieh Tzu passed by, and asked Tai what they were doing. 'We are trying to dig a valley through the mountain, so visitors can visit my house without walking round the mountain.' Lieh Tzu thought for a moment, and then said: 'I suggest that instead of moving the mountain, you move your house. If you were to rebuild it on the other side of the mountain, then a valley would be unnecessary.' Tai was astonished at this suggestion, and immediately began to implement it.

Later Lieh Tzu said to his disciples: 'When you face a problem, reject the most obvious solution, and look for the simplest.'

Chasing the sun

Kua was both strong and nimble, and he prided himself on being the finest fighter in the land. Lieh Tzu passed through the town where Kua lived. Kua heard about the wise man's arrival, and went to see him. 'In all your travels have you ever met a man as strong and nimble as me?' Kua asked. 'Indeed I have not,' replied Lieh Tzu. Kua continued to boast: 'Every person and every animal is terrified of me. If I run towards any living being, that living being runs away in terror.'

Lieh Tzu said: 'Is the sun terrified of you?' Kua puffed out his chest, and said: 'I'm sure the sun is terrified of me.' So Lieh Tzu said: 'You must make good this claim. When the sun is setting tonight, run towards it – and see if you can make it set more quickly.'

So that evening, as the sun was beginning to set in the west, Kua started running towards it. Night fell, and Lieh Tzu and the people of the town went to sleep. The following day Kua returned, utterly exhausted. 'What happened?' Lieh Tzu asked. Kua replied: 'As I ran towards the sun, it refused to set; it remained obstinately in the sky. Only when I collapsed with exhaustion did it finally set.'

Lieh Tzu concluded: 'Your strength and agility have proved worse than useless. Learn to be weak and slow – and then even the sun will respect you.'

Demanding nothing

A nobleman came to Lieh Tzu, and said: 'I want you to teach me the Way, so that I acquire spiritual intelligence. Then I shall be able to appreciate the beauty of all that exists.'

Lieh Tzu replied: 'If you were to follow the Way, you would not demand spiritual intelligence to enable you to appreciate beauty; nor would you demand medicines to maintain the balance of yin and yang within you; nor would you demand food to eat; nor would you demand clothes to wear; nor would you demand a boat with which to cross lakes and rivers. Indeed, you would demand nothing.'

The nobleman looked perplexed. Lieh Tzu concluded: 'You would demand nothing, because you would accept what you are and what you have.'

5

A happy land

Lieh Tzu said to his disciples: 'There is a country where the people are gentle and tolerant, where they never quarrel or argue, and where they are never proud and envious. The old and young live as equals. No one is ruler, and no one is a subject. Men and women mingle freely, making friendships as they wish; and if a man and a woman wish to marry, their families do not need to give permission or exchange expensive gifts. They do not plough the soil, but they eat the fruits and vegetables that grow wild in the forest. There are no epidemics, and they all live their full span. They love to play musical instruments, to sing ballads, and to dance. Their complexions are bright and clear.'

The disciples asked: 'Where is this land?' Lieh Tzu replied: 'It could be any land, even this one, where the people follow the Way.'

Strange customs

Lieh Tzu said to his disciples: 'In the south, where the climate is warm, people cut their hair short, and they wear no clothes. In the north, where the climate is cold, the people wear their hair long, and they clothe themselves in thick furs. In the centre, where the climate is temperate, the people where simple caps and tunics.' The disciples did not react.

Lieh Tzu continued: 'There is a country far to the west where parents cut up their first-born son, and eat him; they say that this makes them more fertile. When a man dies, they carry the widow to the top of a mountain, strip her naked, and leave her to die of cold; they say that a woman should not survive her husband. When young men or women die, they cut the flesh off their bones, and burn it; this is a punishment for premature death. In this country the government approves these customs, and executes anyone who defies them.'

The disciples were shocked to hear of this country. Lieh Tzu smiled, and said: 'You should not find any custom shocking or strange. Human beings are capable of doing the most dreadful things. And once some practice has become customary, people assume it is right.'

5

The size of the sun

Lieh Tzu was travelling in the east of the country, when he saw two children arguing. As the argument was becoming violent, he decided to intervene. 'What are you arguing about?' he asked.

One child said: 'When the sun rises at dawn, it is as big as a shield; but when it sets at dusk, it is as small as a plate.' The other child said: 'When the sun rises at dawn, the air is cold; that proves the sun is small at that time. But when the sun sets at dusk, the air is warm; that proves the sun has grown larger by that time.'

Lieh Tzu said: 'Go to the sun at dawn and at dusk, and measure it with a piece of string.' The first child said: 'The sun at dawn is too far away.' The second child said: 'The sun at dusk is too far away.'

Lieh Tzu concluded: 'Never argue about matters which are beyond your capacity to know.'

5

The lesson of fishing

Lieh Tzu decided to teach himself how to fish. He made a rod and line, and attached a hook and some bait to the end of the line. Then he went down to the river, and threw the line into the water. After a time a large fish took the bait, and was caught on the hook. Lieh Tzu was so excited that he pulled the rod upwards with all his strength. The rod snapped, and the fish got away.

He made another rod and line, and again went down to the river. After a time another large fish took the bait, and was caught on the hook. Lieh Tzu pulled so gently that the fish swam away, pulling the line with him.

Lieh Tzu put another line on his rod, and returned to the river. After a time a third fish took the bait. Lieh Tzu pulled the rod upwards with the same amount of force as the fish was pulling it downwards. So the rod did not break, and the fish could not escape. Eventually, when the fish was utterly exhausted, Lieh Tzu was able to pull it ashore without effort.

That evening Lieh Tzu said to his disciples: 'Today I have learnt an important principle about dealing with the world around you. It is the principle of equality of forces. When the world is pulling you in a particular direction, you should resist its pull with exactly the same degree of force. If you resist too fiercely, you will destroy yourself; if you resist too gently, the world will destroy you.'

Energy and ambition

Kung and Chi lived in the same town, and were close friends. Kung was a wealthy merchant, and Chi was a scholar. One summer they both fell ill.

The town's physician treated them with needles and herbal potions; but both Kung and Chi grew worse. Other physicians from nearby towns were called in; but their efforts failed as well. Finally a message was sent to Lieh Tzu, asking him to come to the town and offer his advice.

Lieh Tzu asked both Kung and Chi many questions. Then he invited them both to see him at the house where he was staying. The two men were carried on stretchers to the house.

Lieh Tzu said to Kung: 'Your problem is that your ambition is greater than your energy. You are ambitious to become the wealthiest man in the town; and you are constantly straining yourself to achieve this ambition. That is why you are ill.' Then he said to Chi: 'Your problem is that your energy is greater than your ambition. You have no ambition to distinguish yourself as a scholar; so you are lazy, and spend much of the day in idleness. That is why you are ill.'

Finally Lieh Tzu said to them both: 'You must each help the other to find the right balance between ambition and energy. Then your health will be restored.'

5

The lute and the birds

A wealthy merchant, who admired Lieh Tzu, gave him a lute. The merchant said: 'I beg you to learn to play this lute, which is the finest in the neighbourhood; your music would bring great joy.' Lieh Tzu had never played a musical instrument, and felt a little daunted; nonetheless he sat under a tree every morning, and taught himself each note.

When he felt proficient, he allowed his fingers to start playing tunes. The tunes were simple and repetitive. But the birds were delighted; they came down from their nests, gathered round Lieh Tzu on the ground, and danced.

One day a young man heard Lieh Tzu play, and saw the birds dancing round him. 'I should like to have command over birds, and make them dance to my tunes,' the young man thought. So he left home, and travelled to the capital city; there he studied music under the finest musician in the land. After three years he could play the lute brilliantly, and had mastered the most complex and powerful tunes that had ever been composed.

The young man returned home, sat under a tree, and started to play. 'Soon the birds will desert Lieh Tzu, and dance round me,' he thought. But not a single bird came to him. Day after day he played; and still the birds stayed away. In desperation he went to Lieh Tzu, and said: 'I have trained for three years, but the birds have no interest in my playing. You have never trained, and yet the birds love your playing.' Lieh Tzu said to the young man: 'Forget all that you have learnt, and then allow your fingers to play as they want.' The young man did so – and the birds gathered round him.

Songs of balance

A young man called Tan came to Lieh Tzu, and asked to study the Way. Lieh Tzu accepted him as a disciple. Whenever Tan did any manual work, he sang the folk songs that he had learnt as a child. Lieh Tzu heard Tan's singing, and realized that he had a fine voice. So he summoned Tan, and said to him: 'I shall teach you the Way through your singing. I want you to come to me each morning, and sing. I shall then advise you how you may attain a finer balance between yin and yang in your voice.' 'How shall I know when my singing has achieved perfect balance?' Tan asked. Lieh Tzu replied: 'At that time the birds will come down from their trees and listen to you.'

So every morning Tan sang for Lieh Tzu, and Lieh Tzu offered advice. After a year of this Tan grew weary, and decided to return home. Lieh Tzu made no objection. He walked with Tan for some distance, until the road passed through a small wood. Then Lieh Tzu said to him: 'Before we part, I should like you to sing once more.' Tan began to sing. The birds in the wood began to sing also; but their notes clashed with Tan's noted, so there was a terrible cacophony.

Tan understood what the birds were expressing. He asked Lieh Tzu if he would take him back as a disciple. Lieh Tzu agreed; and Tan remained with him until his voice had achieved perfect balance between yin and yang.

5

A special gift

Lieh Tzu was walking along a road, when he was overtaken by a young woman. The young woman was singing as she walked. Her voice was utterly enchanting; and Lieh Tzu quickened his pace, so that he could keep up with her.

At dusk the young woman, with Lieh Tzu a few paces behind, reached a small town. The young woman had no money. So she went to an inn, and started to sing. The other travellers enjoyed her singing so much that they bought a meal for her, and paid the innkeeper to provide her with a bed for the night.

The following day Lieh Tzu continued to follow her. That night she went to another inn, to sing for her supper. But before she could open her mouth, the innkeeper asked her if she had any money. 'No,' she replied. 'Another beggar!' he cried, and drove her away.

Lieh Tzu said to her: 'Let your voice teach this cruel man a lesson.' And he instructed her to stand outside the inn, and sing a sad ballad. The other travellers in the inn heard her sing, and were moved to tears. Then the innkeeper himself started to cry. One of the travellers said to him: 'Invite this woman back, and ask her to sing happy songs, so we can be cheerful again.' So the innkeeper invited her back. She sang happy songs; and the innkeeper gave her a meal and a bed for the night.

The following morning Lieh Tzu said to the innkeeper and the other travellers: 'Every person has a special gift, that can make people either happy or sad.'

5

The voice of music

A man called Po came to Lieh Tzu. Po was dumb; but he indicated by gestures that he wished to be a disciple. And Lieh Tzu accepted him.

In a nearby town was a man who made lutes; and Lieh Tzu sent a message to this man, asking him to make a lute for Po. When the lute was complete, Lieh Tzu said to Po: 'Teach yourself to play this, and let it be your voice.' Po devoted every morning and every evening to playing the lute.

Eventually he became proficient. He could express in music every emotion of which the human heart is capable; and he could evoke each emotion in others. When he expressed sadness, his listeners wept; when he expressed joy, his listeners smiled and laughed; when he expressed fear, they trembled; and when he expressed love, they embraced one another.

Lieh Tzu said to him: 'Your music is better than words. When people use words, they are expressing ideas; and they may provoke disagreement and conflict. But since music expresses emotions, no one can disagree, and all feel sympathy.'

5

Hitting the target

One of Lieh Tzu's disciples, called Chi, wished to learn archery. So Lieh Tzu obtained for him a bow and arrows. But Chi proved utterly inept: if he aimed at a tree, his arrow might hit a nearby hedge; if he aimed at a hedge, his arrow might fly past the nose of a nearby cow. Eventually he came to Lieh Tzu in despair, and asked how he could improve.

Lieh Tzu said to him: 'Go to the home of the local weaver, and lie under his loom. As the shuttle passes to and fro in front of your eyes, strive not to blink.' Chi did this for an entire year, and learnt to control his blinking.

He returned to Lieh Tzu, and asked: 'Am I now ready to resume archery?' 'No,' Lieh Tzu replied. 'What else must I do?' Chi asked. Lieh Tzu replied: 'You must catch a flea each day, and attach it to a hair from a yak's tail. As dusk approaches, hang the flea over a window facing west; and watch the flea with the sun behind it.' Chi did this for an entire year. Gradually, month by month, the flea seemed to grow larger, until it was as big as a cartwheel. And when he looked at other objects, they too seemed very large.

He returned to Lieh Tzu, and Lieh Tzu told him he was now ready to resume archery. Chi took his bow with great excitement; and he found he could hit the target with every arrow. When he looked at the target, he could focus his eyes on it without blinking; and it seemed so large that it filled his vision.

5

Controlling horses

One of Lieh Tzu's disciples, called Tai, wished to learn the art of riding a chariot. So Lieh Tzu asked a nobleman, who lived nearby, to lend him one of his many chariots. But Tai proved utterly inept with the reins: when he wanted the horses to gallop, they trotted; and when he wanted them to trot, they galloped. Eventually he came to Lieh Tzu in despair, and asked how he could improve.

Lieh Tzu said to him: 'Set up a row of wooden posts, each one pace apart. Then practice walking along the tops of the posts.' Tai was perplexed at the purpose of this exercise; but he erected twenty posts, and for an entire year he practised walking along them. At first he frequently fell off; but by the end of the year he was able to walk on the posts as if they were solid ground.

He returned to Lieh Tzu, and asked: 'Am I now ready to ride a chariot properly?' Lieh Tzu said: 'Now that you have full control of your own feet, you can control the horses' feet with the reins.' Tai climbed onto the chariot; and he found that he could make the horses gallop and trot as he wanted.

5

Luck and worth

Pei said to Hei: 'I am the same age as you; yet you are re-garded as a success, while I am seen as a failure. We look similar; yet you are admired and loved, while I am ignored. We talk in a similar fashion; yet you are said to be eloquent, while I am said to be coarse and uncouth. We have the same manners; yet people trust you, while they distrust me. When we worked for the same employer, he promoted you, and left me doing the most menial tasks. When we were both mer-chants, people paid a high price for your merchandise, but paid a low price for mine. Thus I wear coarse wool, eat mil-let, lived in a thatched hut, and go about on foot; whereas you wear silks and furs, eat meat, live in a house with a tiled roof, and go about in a carriage drawn by four horses. Worst of all, you treat me with contempt. Do you regard yourself as superior to me?'

Hei replied: 'I have observed, as you have observed, that in every venture I succeed and you fail. I observe, as you ob-serve, that I now live in luxury while you live in poverty. Yet I cannot explain the differences between us. Perhaps the explanation is that I have worked harder than you have; or perhaps from the start I was destined to do better than you. Since I cannot explain the differences, I do not know whether I am superior to you.'

5

Small and large blessings

So Pei and Hei agreed to go to Lieh Tzu, and ask his view. Lieh Tzu questioned them in detail about their respective situations. Then he said: 'Pei has more worth than luck, and Hei has more luck than worth. Pei's failure is not due to folly, and Hei's success is not due to wisdom; success and failure are determined by destiny. Pei's shame and resentment about his failure make him discontent; and Hei's pride and arrogance about his success make him lonely. Let Pei enjoy his small blessings; and let Hei share his large blessings.'

Pei and Hei returned to their respective homes. Pei found that his coarse woollen tunic now felt as warm as fur and as soft as silk; his meals of millet were as tasty as a banquet of the finest meats; and his thatched hut seemed as comfortable as a palace. Hei moved to a smaller house, wore rougher clothes, and ate simpler food; and he gave away much of his wealth. People now regarded him as a friend, and this gave him great happiness.

6

Wisdom and humility

Lieh Tzu said to his disciples: 'Those with greatest wisdom share their spiritual possessions with others. Those next in wisdom share their material possessions with others.

'Those who pride themselves on their wisdom, look down on those who are humble. But other people do not listen to those who regard themselves as wise; they are more inclined to listen to those who are humble.

'Those possessing both wisdom and humility enjoy the highest respect of all.'

6

Illness and treatment

A wealthy merchant called Chu fell ill. He was sceptical about physicians, and at first refused to call one. But after seven days his illness reached a crisis; and his family insisted on calling a physician. The physician examined Chu, and then declared: 'Your illness is caused by irregular meals, excessive sexual activity, and anxiety about your business. Therefore if you eat regularly, abstain from sex, and give up your business, you will be cured.' Despite his weakness Chu shouted: 'You're a fool! Get out of my house!'

Chu's family called a second physician, who examined Chu, and declared: 'Your illness was caused by receiving too little vital fluid in your mother's womb, and too much milk at your mother's breast. So it cannot be cured.' Chu shouted: 'You're intelligent. Stay for dinner.'

Chu's family now called Lieh Tzu, who said: 'In rejecting treatment you increase the likelihood of dying from this illness; but you also demonstrate your indifference to whether you live or die. Therefore folly and wisdom are equally balanced in you.'

Chu was astonished at Lieh Tzu's words. He called the finest physician in the region; and under this physician's treatment he quickly recovered.

6

Two brothers

Two brothers, who were now old men, came to Lieh Tzu. They were identical twins. One of them said to Lieh Tzu: 'As you can see, we are the same in age, appearance, manner of speaking and natural abilities.' The other added: 'Yet we are utterly different in status, wealth and respect. I have been highly successful, while my brother has failed in every venture he has attempted.' They asked Lieh Tzu to explain this.

Lieh Tzu said: 'There are many events that have no rational explanation; they are due to destiny. Many things occur in people's lives that are unconnected with how they act; these things are due to destiny. So for those who embrace destiny, there is no difference between success and failure, between a long life and a short one, between riches and poverty, and between honour and dishonour.'

6

Attitudes and aptitudes

Lieh Tzu said to his disciples: 'One person may be cautious, another impetuous; but both can be wise. One person may be lethargic, another energetic; but both can be effective. One person may be devious, another simple; but both can achieve their purposes. One person may be blunt, another adept at flattery; but both can be likeable. One person may be eloquent, another tongue-tied; but both can be understood by those who listen. One person may be jolly, another serious; but both can be happy. One person may prefer company, another may prefer solitude; but both can be content.

'Every person is a complex mixture of attitudes and aptitudes; no two people are the same. But no one is barred from following the Way.'

6

A beautiful mansion

A nobleman called Ching lived in a large mansion, which was situated in a beautiful valley. He admired Lieh Tzu, and invited him to stay in his mansion. One morning Lieh Tzu suggested that they climb one of the hills overlooking the valley. So the two men set out, accompanied by several of Ching's servants.

Ching was old, so they walked slowly. When they finally reached the top of the hill, they sat down, and looked over the valley and the mansion. Tears welled up in Ching's eyes. 'Why are you weeping?' Lieh Tzu asked. The nobleman replied: 'Soon I shall die – and I shall depart from this beautiful place. If only I could stay alive for ever!' One of his servants echoed his sentiments: 'We too love this place so much that we dread the prospect of death.'

Lieh Tzu smiled, and said: 'Let us imagine that your father, grandfather, great-grandfather, and all your ancestors had remained alive. The mansion would now be packed with them, and there would be no space for you. So, far from enjoying its splendour and comfort, you would be working in a rice field and living in a thatched hut. You must die in order that your descendents can have their turn.'

A few years later Ching caught a fatal illness. He remembered Lieh Tzu's, and was content to die.

The loss of a son

Wu and his wife had a son whom they loved dearly. At the age of twenty this son fell down a well and died. Wu and his wife were overcome with grief.

As the weeks and months passed Wu's wife became calm, and she was able to resume her normal activities. But Wu continued to grieve. During the day he sat in his house, and wept; and during the night he walked through the nearby forest, beating his fists against the trees. He failed to sow seeds in the spring, and his fields were overrun with weeds. His wife tried to comfort him, but her words and embraces merely deepened his sadness. So she sent a message to Lieh Tzu, begging him to come and speak to her husband.

Lieh Tzu said to Wu: 'Cast your mind back forty years to your own childhood.' Wu did so; and his mind filled with memories of himself and his friends playing games. Then Lieh Tzu said: 'Cast your mind back twenty-five years, to the time when you and your wife first married.' Wu did so; and his mind filled with memories of new love.

Lieh Tzu concluded: 'In those days you had no son, and now once again you have no son.' Wu stopped grieving, and went to his fields to pull up weeds.

6

The nature of professions

Lieh Tzu said to his disciples: 'Farmers hurry to keep up with the seasons. Merchants chase after profits. Craftsmen strive to improve their skills. Officials pursue power. This is the nature of their professions.

'But from time to time farmers face droughts and floods. On some deals merchants make losses. Craftsmen sometimes make mistakes that ruin their work. Officials are always in danger of incurring the king's displeasure, so that he demotes them. Failure occurs in every profession.

'Constant success cannot be ensured; and occasional failure cannot be avoided.'

6

Following the shadow

A disciple called Hu was constantly active; from the moment he awoke to the moment he fell asleep he did useful tasks. As a result his body was constantly tense, his flesh was wasting away, and he was frequently ill.

So Lieh Tzu summoned Hu, and said to him: 'Look at your shadow.' Hu looked at his shadow. 'What is your shadow doing?' Lieh asked. Hu replied: 'It is doing what I am doing – sitting and talking to you.' 'Does your shadow follow you in everything you do?' Lieh Tzu asked. 'Yes, of course,' Hu answered. 'So you are the master and your shadow is the servant,' Lieh Tzu said. 'Yes,' Hu replied

Lieh Tzu said: 'From now onwards, from the middle of the day until the evening, you must be the servant and your shadow the master. Follow your shadow in everything it does.'

Since his shadow had no power to act on its own, Hu was forced to remain still throughout every afternoon. As a result his body became relaxed, his flesh was restored, and he enjoyed good health.

8

Echo and shadow

Lieh Tzu said to his disciples: 'If your voice is loud, its echo is loud; if your voice is soft, its echo is soft. If you are tall in stature, your shadow is tall; if you are short in stature, your shadow is short.

'Friendship and enmity are the echoes of action; love and hatred are the shadows of action. If your actions are kind, then their echo is friendship; if your actions are cruel, then their echo is enmity. If your conduct is generous, the shadow is love; if your conduct is mean, the shadow is hatred.'

8

Hitting the target

A disciple called Kuan decided to learn archery. He quickly acquired the skill, so that with every shot he hit the target.

Lieh Tzu asked him: 'Do you know how you hit the target?' Kuan replied: 'No. I simply shoot the arrow to the best of my ability.' Lieh Tzu said: 'Until you understand how you hit the target, you have not truly learnt archery.' So Kuan strove to understand how he hit the target.

After three years he returned to Lieh Tzu, and said: 'I now know how I hit the target.' Lieh Tzu replied: 'Hold onto that knowledge, and don't lose it.'

8

White hair

Lieh Tzu said to his disciples: 'Those in the prime of their beauty are proud; those in the prime of their strength are impetuous. So you cannot talk to people in their prime about the Way. People with no white streaks in their hair have difficulty understanding the Way, and even greater difficulty following it. If people are proud and impetuous, they are interested only in the acquisition of wealth, power and status.

'Wise people are happy to give authority to others. So their capacity does not diminish with age; nor is it limited by the limits of their own knowledge. A wise king can rule effectively until he dies. Wise merchants can buy and sell effectively until they die. Wise farmers can till the soil and raise livestock effectively until they die. Wise teachers can teach effectively until they die.'

8

The jade leaf

A craftsman carved a model of a mulberry leaf out of jade. The task took him three years. Its shape, veins, colour and lustre were identical to those of a real mulberry leaf; so when it was put amongst real leaves, no one could spot it. The craftsman presented the model leaf to the king. The king was so pleased that he rewarded the craftsman with a salary and a house.

When Lieh Tzu heard about the craftsman's work and reward, he said: 'If the soil was so slow that it took three years to produce a leaf, trees would be almost bare. Let human beings do what they are destined to do.'

8

An unwelcome gift

At one time Lieh Tzu was short of funds, and he and his wife grew very thin. A visitor mentioned this to the chief minister, and added: 'Lieh Tzu is well known as a man of wisdom. If you were to become his patron, you would win great respect.'

The chief minister immediately arranged for a messenger to take a large quantity of grain to Lieh Tzu. When the messenger arrived, Lieh Tzu refused the gift. His wife was distraught, and cried: 'Starvation is staring at us; surely you can swallow your pride and accept this food with gratitude.'

Lieh Tzu replied: 'It's not pride that prevents me from accepting it, but wisdom. The chief minister does not know me personally, but sent me this grain on the word of someone else. Equally he may condemn me on the word of someone else. That is why I refuse the gift.'

8

Fathers and sons

Shih had two sons; one was scholarly, and the other was interested in military matters. The first son went to a small kingdom, where the king employed him as his advisor on morality. The other went to a large kingdom, where the king employed him as his military advisor. Shih was proud of his sons' success.

Meng also had two sons; one was scholarly, and the other was interested in military matters. Observing the success of Shih's sons, Meng told his sons to imitate them. The first son went to the large kingdom, and offered himself as advisor on moral matters. The king said: 'I am engaged in constant warfare, as I strive to extend my kingdom; I have no time to concern myself with morality.' So he sent the young man away. The second son went to the small kingdom, and offered himself as military advisor. The king said: 'My kingdom is weak, so I never engage in war. Instead I strive to act with honour, in order to win the favour of my stronger neighbours.' So he sent the young man away.

Meng was bitterly disappointed. He went to Lieh Tzu, and said: 'My sons are equal in ability to Shih's sons. So why have his sons succeeded, while my sons have failed?' Lieh Tzu replied: 'Ability is only a minor factor in determining success or failure. Fortune is the greater factor. Shih's sons had good fortune, and your sons had bad fortune.'

Nearby attractions

A certain king taxed his people heavily, in order to assemble a large army; his purpose was to conquer a neighbouring kingdom, and add it to his own. The heavy taxes made his people poor and miserable.

Lieh Tzu travelled through this kingdom, and saw the people's plight. He went to the king, and said: 'There was once a man, who was walking along a lane with his wife. He spotted an attractive young woman picking fruit nearby, and went to talk to her. But when he looked round, he saw another man talking to his wife.'

The king understood his meaning. He dismissed his army, lowered taxes, and devoted himself to the welfare of his people.

8

Death of a detective

A certain kingdom was infested with robbers. Hung was able to read a person's face, so he could pick out robbers merely by looking at them. The king heard about Hung, and decided to employ him as a detective. So Hung began to travel round the kingdom, identifying those who had committed crimes; he was followed by soldiers, who arrested the criminals.

When Lieh Tzu heard about Hung's activities, he went to the king, and said: 'You can never rid your kingdom of robbers merely by identifying them and arresting them. Besides, you have condemned Hung to an early death.' The king refused to listen; nor did he ask Lieh Tzu's advice on defeating crime.

The bands of robbers now came together, and formed an army. As Hung and the soldiers were going through a valley, the army of robbers attacked and killed them. When the king heard the news, he remembered Lieh Tzu's words, and summoned him to his palace.

Lieh Tzu said: 'Detection and punishment can never succeed. The only means of defeating crime is to instil shame in people's hearts, so they no longer want to be criminals. Thus you must appoint to high office people renowned for their honesty. They will appoint people of honesty to lower offices. Thus a spirit of honesty will gradually spread through the land – and then crime will cease.'

8

Crossing a river

A nobleman arrived, with his retinue of guards and servants, at a river. There was a ford, which normally was easy to cross. But there had been heavy rains during the previous month, so the river was high and fast. As the nobleman was wondering what to do, Lieh Tzu arrived on the opposite side.

Without hesitation Lieh Tzu walked down the bank and into the water. The nobleman was astonished. Lieh Tzu soon disappeared beneath the foam, and the nobleman assumed he had drowned. But a short time later Lieh Tzu emerged from the water some distance downstream.

The nobleman rode along the bank, and asked Lieh Tzu if he possessed some special skill. Lieh Tzu replied: 'I possess no special skill. I simply throw my body into the current. If I were to resist the water, it would drown me. But since I respect the water, it carries me.'

The nobleman did not dare follow Lieh Tzu's example, and turned back.

8

Hidden treasure

A robber, who possessed many stolen gems and coins, asked
Lieh Tzu: 'Is it possible to hide something, so that no one
else can find it.' Lieh Tzu did not reply. The robber persisted: 'Could I hide a stone by throwing it into a deep lake?'
Lieh Tzu replied: 'A good diver could find it.' The robber
asked: 'Could I hide some water by pouring it into a lake.'
Lieh Tzu replied: 'A person of astute taste could find it.' 'So
can nothing be hidden?' the robber asked.

Lieh Tzu replied: 'No material thing can be hidden. Only
truth is hidden; it is veiled by the words that wise people
utter. But if you study that veil with care, you will eventually
see through it.'

The robber went home, put the stolen gems and coins
into a sack, and took them back to their owners. Then he returned to Lieh Tzu, and became a disciple.

8

Premature celebrations

A king decided that he wished to expand his kingdom; so he attacked a city in a neighbouring kingdom. After several days of fierce fighting his soldiers were victorious. The king celebrated for several days. He arranged grand banquets in the city hall for himself and his noblemen, and he ordered the musicians and dancers of the city to entertain them.

Lieh Tzu heard about these celebrations, and went to the defeated city. He walked into the city hall, and said to the king: 'Your celebrations are premature. You may have defeated the city's army, but you have not won its people.' 'What do you mean?' the king asked. Lieh Tzu answered: 'This city will not be part of your kingdom until its people acknowledge you as their king.'

The king dismissed Lieh Tzu, and continued to eat and drink. A short time later a large crowd of people burst into the hall, and killed him and all his noblemen.

8

White calves

A family was renowned for the virtuous conduct of all its members. It owned a black cow; and, for no apparent reason, the cow gave birth to a white calf. The family asked Lieh Tzu to explain this. 'It is a good omen,' Lieh Tzu replied. A few months later the father went blind.

A year later the cow again gave birth to another white calf. Again the family asked Lieh Tzu to explain this. 'It is a good omen,' Lieh Tzu replied. A few months later the eldest son went blind.

A year later the cow gave birth to a third white calf. The father said: 'Let us again ask Lieh Tzu about this.' The son replied: 'No, let us ignore Lieh Tzu. He said the first white calf was a good omen, and you went blind. He said the second calf was a good omen, and I went blind.' The father said: 'The words of wise people may seem at first to be proved wrong, but eventually they are proved right.' So they asked Lieh Tzu to explain the third white calf; and again he said it was a good omen.

Soon afterwards the region was attacked by the king of a neighbouring country. The able-bodied men formed an army to resist the attack; and many were killed and injured. But the father and the son of the virtuous family could not fight, and so they were unharmed.

A few months later the father and the son regained their sight.

A juggler and a dancer

A young man taught himself to walk on stilts. Then he taught himself to juggle. And finally he taught himself to walk on stilts and juggle at the same time.

He went to the royal palace, and performed in front of the king. He walked forwards and backwards on stilts, while juggling seven swords. The king was so impressed that he gave the young man a bag of gold coins.

Hearing of this young man's success, another young man taught himself to dance on the back of a horse, while the horse galloped in circles. He too went to the royal palace, and asked to perform in front of the king. But the king ordered him to leave, and never return.

This second young man went to see Lieh Tzu, and told him what had happened. Lieh Tzu said: 'The first young man had no thought of a reward; so he was rewarded. But you thought only of a reward; so you were not rewarded.'

8

Youthful ambition

A young man called Sun, who was exceptionally intelligent, came to see Lieh Tzu. He said: 'I wish to win the highest reputation, wield the greatest power, and accumulate the most wealth that my intelligence will allow.'

Lieh Tzu said to him: 'If your reputation is high, others will resent you. If your power is great, others will hate you. If your wealth is large, others will envy you.' The young man asked: 'What must I do to avoid resentment, hatred and envy?'

Lieh Tzu replied: 'The higher your reputation, the humbler you must become. The greater your power, the gentler you must become. The larger your wealth, the more generous you must become.'

8

Remote land

Shu was a man of great virtue. The king liked and admired him, and offered him some land. It was rich and fertile; and its crops could easily be transported to the capital city, since it lay near the road that ran from the city to the border. So its owner would soon become wealthy.

Shu went to Lieh Tzu, and asked whether he should accept the king's offer. Lieh Tzu replied: 'Whenever this kingdom is invaded, soldiers march across that land. Ask the king to give you land far away from the capital city and the border.'

Shu took Lieh Tzu's advice; and the king gave him land in the shadow of a remote mountain range. Shu's family lived safely on that land for many generations; and although they never became rich, they always had enough.

8

Reactions to robbers

Ni took pride in his wisdom and in his calmness. Early one morning a band of robbers broke into his house, and loaded all his possessions into sacks. He showed no signs of distress, and did nothing to resist them. As the robbers were preparing to leave, they asked him to explain his attitude. Ni replied: 'A wise man doesn't risk his life for the sake of possessions, which are only the means of supporting life.' The leader of the robbers said to the others: 'This man is so calm that he has observed our faces closely. If we don't kill him, he'll point us out to the constables.' So the robbers stabbed him with their knives, and he died.

Lieh Tzu heard about Ni's fate. Some time later a band of robbers broke into his house, and loaded all his possessions into sacks. He made a feeble effort to resist them. Then he grabbed his wife, and pulled her into a corner; and with their faces to the wall they pretended to weep. The robbers left the house without harming them.

8

Death for a king

A man called Chu served a king called Ao. He came to feel that Ao did not appreciate him. So he resigned, and went to live on the seashore, where he ate whatever nuts and seeds he could find.

But after some time news came to Chu that a neighbouring king was attacking King Ao. Chu decided to return to Ao, and fight in his army. When he reached Ao's palace, his old friends were astonished to see him. One of them said: 'You left Ao because you felt he did not appreciate you; yet now you are willing to die for him. We cannot understand you.' Chu replied: 'If I die in his army, Ao will feel utterly ashamed at the way he treated me; and his shame will haunt him for the rest of his life.'

Chu fought bravely, and helped Ao to defeat his enemy; and in the course of the fighting he was killed. As he had anticipated, Ao was utterly ashamed; and this shame persisted for months and years. Finally in desperation he summoned Lieh Tzu, and asked his advice. Lieh Tzu said: 'Let your shame turn to respect. He refused to serve a master who did not appreciate him; and he died for a master who did appreciate him. Thus without doubt he followed the Way.'

8

YANG CHU

The deeds and sayings of Yang Chu are entirely contained in the sixth and eighth chapters of the book of Lieh Tzu – although it is possible these originally formed a separate book. He lived in the third century BCE, and probably came from a wealthy family. He seems to have had both a wife and a concubine, which was a common arrangement for gentlemen in this period. But as a scholar and a sage he chose to live simply. He accumulated a body of disciples.

The mean employer

Yang Chu arrived at a large town, and found the people there very unhappy. He asked the reason for their unhappiness. They told him that a man called Wan ran most of the workshops in the town, farmed most of the nearby land, and thus employed most of the able-bodied men; and that Wan paid low wages and demanded hard work.

So Yang Chu went to see Wan, and said: 'You are extremely rich. But what use is wealth?' Wan replied: 'Wealth enables me to exert power over others.' Yang Chu asked: 'And what use is power over others?' Wan replied: 'They fear me.' Yang Chu asked: 'And what use is being regarded with fear?' Wan replied: 'They obey my orders.' Yang Chu asked: 'And what use is obedience?' Wan replied: 'They will work as I want.' Lieh Tzu: 'And what use is such work?' Wan replied: 'It makes me rich.'

That evening Wan reflected on this conversation, and realized how foolish he was. So from the next day onwards he paid high wages, and allowed people to work as their strength and abilities allowed.

6

Opposite moods

The king appointed a man called Kuan as chief minister. After a few months as chief minister, Kuan came to Yang Chu, and said: 'The king is sometimes cautious and sometimes brave; sometimes calm and sometimes anxious; sometimes gentle and sometimes firm. How should I respond to his changing moods?' Yang Chu replied: 'You have a choice: either you can adapt your mood to his; or you can make your mood the opposite to his. If you take the former choice, you will benefit; if you take the latter choice, your family will benefit.'

Kuan loved his family dearly, so he decided to make his mood the opposite of the king's. When the king was brave, he was cautious; and when the king was cautious, he was brave. When the king was anxious, he was calm; and when the king was calm, he was anxious. When the king was firm, he was gentle; and when the king was gentle, he was firm. As a result they acted together with moderation, and so ruled with great wisdom.

The king, however, grew weary of his chief minister having the opposite mood to his; he accused Kuan of being perverse. Kuan admitted that he altered his moods deliberately; so the king beheaded him. But the people remembered Kuan with gratitude; as a result they treated his family with great respect and generosity.

6

Similar moods

After beheading Kuan, the king appointed Heng as his chief minister. After a few months as chief minister, Heng came to Yang Chu, and said: 'The king is sometimes cautious and sometimes brave; sometimes calm and sometimes anxious; sometimes gentle and sometimes firm. How should I respond to his changing moods?' Yang Chu replied: 'You have a choice: either you can adapt your mood to his; or you can make your mood the opposite to his. If you take the former choice, you will benefit; if you take the latter choice, your family will benefit.'

Heng was ambitious, so he decided to adapt his moods to the king's. When the king was brave, he was brave; and when the king was cautious, he was cautious. When the king was anxious, he was anxious; and when the king was calm, he was calm. When the king was firm, he was firm; and when the king was gentle, he was gentle. As a result their actions were extreme, and they ruled with great folly.

The king, however, was delighted that his chief minister was in such close sympathy with him, and gave him a grand mansion in which to live. Heng eventually died; and the people were delighted. The king took back the mansion, and Heng's family were forced to live in poverty.

6

A young man's aim

A young man came to Yang Chu, and said: 'My parents are ambitious for me; they want me to pursue success in my life. Should I obey my parents in this?' Yang Chu replied: 'Let us assume that you live your full span. You have already spent a quarter of that time in childhood, when you are too young to achieve success; and you will spend almost another quarter too old and weak to achieve success. A third of your time is spent asleep, when you can do nothing; and when you are awake, you must spend some time at rest. Eating and drinking absorbs more time. And you fall sick occasionally. So there is very little time left for success.'

The young man said: 'Should I pursue pleasure instead? Should my aim be to eat delicious food, wear silks and brocades, listen to sweet music, and surround myself with beautiful women?' Yang Chu replied: 'If pleasure is your aim, you will constantly be seeking the means of pleasure – the food, the clothes, the music and the women. So there will be very little time for enjoyment.'

The young man said: 'Should a high reputation be my aim?' Yang Chu replied: 'If you pursue reputation, you will become the slave of those whose respect you seek. You will constantly try to say what they want you to say, and do what they want you to do.'

'So what should my aim be?' the young man asked. Yang Chu replied: 'Your aim should be to have no aim.'

The king and his groom

Yang Chu said to his disciples: 'In life all living beings are different from one another; in death they are the same. In life some people are clever, and some are stupid; some are wise, and some are foolish; some are noble, and some are vile. But in death all people decay, and turn into dust.

'Some will die in ten years time, and some will die in a hundred years time; but all will die at some time. In life one man is a king, and another man grooms his horses; one woman is a princess, and another makes her clothes. But in death they are equal. Can you tell the bones of a king from the bones of his groom; can you tell the bones of a princess from the bones of her seamstress?

'So do not waste your life aspiring to be what you are not. Accept life as it is, and enjoy it.'

6

Beggars in a mansion

Yuan was the poorest person in a certain town. He dressed in rags, so in the winter he shivered with cold; he begged for scraps of food, so he was constantly hungry. He frequently said to himself: 'No one in this town can be more miserable than I am.'

Kung was the richest person in the town. His mansion was filled with gold ornaments and precious stones; and he was so anxious that thieves might break in, that at night he lay awake. His cooks fed him large amounts of the finest food; thus he was so fat he could barely walk, and he suffered chronic indigestion. He frequently said to himself: 'No one in this town can be more miserable than I am.'

Yang Chu travelled through the town, and met Yuan in the street. Yuan told him of his plight. 'Who is the richest person in this town?' Yang Chu asked. Yuan replied that Kung was the richest man, and directed him to Kung's mansion.

Yang Chu visited Kung, and Kung told him of his plight. 'I can make you happy and healthy,' Yang Chu said to him. 'Do whatever is necessary,' Kung replied. Yang Chu fetched Yuan and the other beggars in the town, and he brought them to live in Kung's house. The beggars took it in turns to guard the mansion at night; and they shared the food that the cooks provided.

Kung could now sleep at night; and he lost weight, so he could walk at a normal pace and digest food easily. And Yuan and the other beggars had full bellies and warm bodies.

The living and the dead

Yang Chu said to his disciples: 'There is an old saying that each of us should have compassion on the living, and abandon the dead.

'In order to have compassion on the living, you should not merely feel for them. When you see people toiling so hard that they are collapsing with exhaustion, you go to assist them in their work. When you see people hungry, you give them food. When you see people cold, you give them warm clothes, and wood to make a fire. When you see people in any kind of trouble, you help them.

'In order to abandon the dead, you should not merely refuse to feel sorry for them. You should not put pearls or jade in their mouths, or dress them in silks and brocades, or prepare funeral vessels.'

6

Nurturing life

A man called Chung asked Yang Chu how to nurture life. Yang Chu replied: 'Live without restraint: suppress nothing, and restrict nothing.' 'Tell me more,' the man asked.

Yang Chu replied: 'Give your ears to whatever they enjoy hearing. Give your eyes to whatever they enjoy seeing. Give your nostrils to whatever they enjoy smelling. Give your mouth to whatever it enjoys saying. Give your body to whatever makes it comfortable. Give your will to whatever it wishes to achieve.

'If your ears wish to hear music, and you close your ears to music, then you are suppressing your ears. If your eyes wish to see beautiful women, and you avert your eyes from beautiful women, then you are suppressing your eyes. If your nostrils wish to smell orchids and spices, and you turn away from orchids and spices, then you are suppressing your nostrils. If your mouth wishes to discuss truth and falsehood, and you remain silent, you are restricting your intelligence. If your body enjoys consuming particular foods and dressing in particular clothes, and you deny it that food and those clothes, you are restricting your comfort. If your will yearns for freedom, and you live in servitude, you are restricting your own nature.

'All restrictions are tyrants. If you can overthrow these tyrants, then you will nurture life.'

Taking leave of the dead

Chung now said to Yang Chu: 'You have told me about nurturing life. Now tell me about taking leave of the dead?' Yang Chu replied: 'It doesn't matter how we take leave of the dead. What is there to say about it?' Chung insisted: 'I should like to hear your thoughts on it.'

Yang Chu replied: 'Once I am dead, the disposal of my body is no concern of mine. My body may be burnt on a fire, or thrown into a river. It may be buried in the ground, or left in the open for the birds and wild animals to eat. It may be thrown into a ditch and covered with grass, or it may be put in a stone coffin dressed in a jacket embroidered with a dragon. I am happy to leave the disposal of my body to others.'

Chung thanked Yang Chu, and said: 'You have told me all I need to know about nurturing life and taking leave of the dead.'

6

The wisdom of wine and women

The king appointed a man called Chan as his chief minister. Within three years Chan had imposed order on the kingdom: the good felt secure, while the wicked lived in fear. Chan felt immensely proud of his success; but he worked so hard that he enjoyed no pleasure.

Chan had an elder brother called Chao, who was fond of wine and was frequently drunk. And he had a younger brother called Mu, who was fond of beautiful young women, and frequently seduced young virgins for his own pleasure. Chan felt ashamed of his brothers, fearing that their unruly behaviour would bring disgrace upon him.

So he went to Chao and Mu, and said: 'If you were to restrain your appetites, I should appoint you both to high office, and you would be treated by others with respect. But if you continue to indulge your appetites, you will destroy your health, and be regarded by others with contempt.'

Chao replied: 'Life is precious and short; so we wish to enjoy it to the full while it lasts. When my belly grows too weak for wine, I shall be happy to die.' Mu added: 'You are not concerned for our reputations, but for your own. When my potency grows too weak to satisfy my lust, I shall be happy to die.'

Chan went to Yang Chu, and asked his advice. Yang Chu said: 'In your brothers' folly there is wisdom. In your wisdom there is folly. Let them be foolish in their own wise fashion. And continue to be wise in your own foolish fashion.'

6

Pleasure and contentment

When he was a young man, Tuan inherited a large mansion, a huge estate, and ten thousand pieces of gold. From that day onwards he ignored the affairs of the world, and indulged his desires. If he wanted a particular dish, he ordered his cooks to prepare it. If he wanted a certain wine, he ordered his servants to bring it from his cellar. If he wanted to hear a favourite melody, he ordered his musicians to play it. If he wanted to visit some beautiful place, he arranged for his carriage to take him there.

At the age of fifty he found that his desires were fading and his capacity for pleasure diminishing; and by the age of sixty his wealth gave him no pleasure at all. So he went to Yang Chu, and asked what he should do. Yang Chu said: 'By means of indulging your desires, you have become free from desire. By means of folly you have become wise. Hand your mansion, your estate and your gold to your sons and daughters; then go and live in a simple hut, eat simple food, drink water from a stream, listen to the birds, and do not travel. You will be perfectly content; and you will find that contentment is superior to pleasure.'

6

The quantity and quality of experience

A man called Sung came to Yang Chu, and asked: 'If I were to eat only the right food, drink only the right liquids, and refrain from every kind of harmful or dangerous activity, would I live for ever?' Yang Chu replied: 'It is impossible to live for ever.'

'Would I prolong my life?' Sung asked. Yang Chu replied: 'It is impossible to prolong life. Besides what is the point of prolonging life? The pleasures of the future are the same as those of the past. The problems of the future are the same as those of the past. The joys of the future are the same as those of the past. The worries of the future are the same as those of the past. So if you live until the age of a hundred, you will experience nothing new; the quantity of experience will grow, but the quality will remain unchanged.'

Sung said: 'If that is so, should I not destroy myself now by falling on a spear, rushing into a fire, or diving into boiling water?' Yang Chu replied: 'No. Let life run its course, and satisfy your desires. And when it is time to die, let death run its course. Let everything run its course at its own pace.'

6

A single hair

A young man called Kuli, who took pride in his own cleverness, asked Yang Chu: 'If you could help the whole world by sacrificing one hair on your body, would you do it?' Yang Chu replied: 'The world would certainly not be helped by one hair.' Kuli persisted: 'But supposing it would be helped, would you do it?'

Yang Chu said: 'Let me first ask you some questions. If you could win ten thousand gold coins by piercing your skin, would you do it?' Without hesitation Kuli said: 'Yes.' Yang Chu asked: 'If you could gain a whole kingdom by cutting off your legs, would you do it?' Kuli hesitated.

Yang Chu said: 'One hair is a trifle compared with an injury to the flesh; and an injury to the flesh is a trifle compared with the loss of limbs. Yet enough hairs are worth as much as a piece of flesh; and enough flesh is worth as much as a limb. So we should not treat a single hair lightly; everything matters.'

6

A single sheep and a flock

The king's wife refused to obey him, and did whatever she wanted; and his concubine mocked him, and called him rude names. This disobedience and mockery destroyed his self-respect, and he felt unable to rule his kingdom. So he invited Yang Chu to his palace, told him of his plight, and asked his advice.

Yang Chu said to him: 'Think of a boy tending sheep. If he has a flock of a hundred sheep, he can control them easily. When he waves his stick to the east, the sheep go eastwards; when he waves his stick to the west, the sheep go westwards. But if he has a single sheep, he is unable to control it. He can wave his stick in any direction, but the sheep will only go where it wants. You are unable to control your wife, and you are unable to control your concubine, because each is like a single sheep. But you can still control the kingdom, because it is like a flock.'

6

Memories and records

Yang Chu said to his disciples: 'Most of the events of the recent past have been forgotten; only a few are remembered, and even fewer have been recorded. All the events of the distant past have been forgotten. Consider ten years ago: out of a million events, a hundred are remembered and ten are recorded. Consider a hundred years ago: out of a million events, none is remembered, and one is recorded. Consider a thousand or ten thousand years ago: no events are remembered, and no events are recorded. Every wise word and every foolish word, every good action and every wicked action, every beautiful face and every ugly face, fades and vanishes.

'Yet human beings strive to say something or do something that will be remembered after their death. How vain and how foolish!'

6

The mind and the body

Yang Chu said to his disciples: 'Human beings have the most intelligent minds of all living beings on earth. But our nails and teeth are not strong enough to defend ourselves. Our skin and flesh are too soft to provide protection. We cannot run fast enough to escape danger. We lack fur and feathers to insulate us against the cold. Thus, unlike other living beings, we depend on our minds for the survival of our bodies.

'I do not own my body; yet once I have been born, I have no choice but to try and preserve it. I own nothing; yet once I exist, my body depends on many things for its preservation. The body is not life, but it is the means by which we live.

'Foolish people, who use their minds badly, think they own their bodies; and they strive to take possession of the things on which the body depends. As a result they live in constant fear of attack. Wise people, who use their minds well, know that they have been lent a body for a period, and they receive as gifts the things on which the body depends.'

6

The anxiety of folly

Yang Chu said to his disciples: 'Foolish people want wealth, power and status. They are willing to exploit others in their quest for wealth. They are willing to oppress others in their quest for power. And they are willing to slander others in their quest for status. They are also desperate to live their full span, so they can enjoy the fruits of their exploitation, oppression and slander.

'As a result they never rest, and are constantly anxious. Before they have wealth, power and status, they strive day and night to obtain them. After they have wealth, power and status, they strive day and night to protect them from others. And they never stop worrying about the state of their bodily health.

'Wise people accept whatever destiny provides, and want nothing apart from what destiny provides. They are thus in harmony with anything and everything.'

6

The king and the farmer

From time to time the king rode out into the countryside, and observed the men and women tilling the soil and tending their flocks. One day the king climbed down from his carriage, and spoke to a man called Sung. 'Are you happy with your way of life?' the king asked. The man replied: 'Of course I am happy. By working hard each day on the land my joints remain supple and my muscles vigorous. And when I return to my cottage in the evening, I am ravenous; so the beans and millet, which my wife has prepared, are like a banquet. My body is so strong and healthy that I rarely fall ill, and in winter I can hardly feel the cold.'

When the king returned to his palace, he was filled with envy for Sung. He thought: 'My work requires me to sit for most of the day, so my joints have become stiff and my muscles slack. My appetite is poor, and I need the finest food to stimulate it. In winter I have to wear soft furs and have blazing fires in every room, in order to keep warm; and I frequently catch chills. The life of a humble farmer is far superior to that of a king.'

His envy prevented him from concentrating on the problems that his ministers brought to him. And soon the kingdom was falling into disorder.

6

Swapping places

Rumours began to spread of the king's condition, and Yang Chu went to visit him. The king told Yang Chu about his meeting with Sung, a humble farmer, and described Sung's way of life. He concluded: 'I am filled with envy for Sung, and as a result I no longer care about my kingdom.' Yang Chu said: 'Swap places with Sung for a month, so that he lives in this palace, while you till the soil.'

The following morning the king, accompanied by his wife, went to Sung, and put Yang Chu's suggestion to him. Sung and his wife were delighted. But within a few days the king, Sung, and their wives were utterly miserable. Tilling the soil caused every muscle and joint in the king's body to ache; and handling tools caused the skin of his hands to blister. Neither he nor his wife could digest millet and beans, so the flesh on their bodies began to waste away. And the cold winds at night penetrated their bones, so they could hardly sleep. Meanwhile in the king's palace Sung and his wife found the food excessively rich, and vomited after every meal; and the lack of manual activity made their bodies tense, so they too could hardly sleep.

At the end of the month the king and his wife, and Sung and his wife, were overjoyed to return to their respective homes. And the king dedicated himself to the tasks of ruling the kingdom with greater vigour than ever before.

6

The stolen sheep

A farmer called Hu had a large flock of sheep. One day he found that one of his sheep was missing, and he assumed that a thief had stolen it. Although the loss of a single sheep hardly affected him, he was consumed by fury. He gathered all his servants, and they set out along the road in pursuit. After some distance they came to a fork in the road; half the group went in one direction, and half in the other. Then each group came to a further fork, and they divided again. At each fork the groups divided in two, so eventually there was only one man on each road. And when this man reached a further fork, he gave up in despair, and returned home.

Some months later Yang Chu passed through this neighbourhood. He saw Hu, and noticed that his face was red. He asked Hu the reason. Hu told him that he was still angry at the loss of a sheep; and he recounted his futile efforts to catch the thief. Yang Chu said: 'Your efforts were far from futile; you learnt a valuable lesson. You and your servants tried to go in all directions, just as ambitious people try to satisfy all their desires. But eventually you were forced to return to where you started – just as wise people return to the soul, where life starts.'

Hu's anger subsided, and he began to follow the Way.

To drown or to swim

Three brothers had a bitter argument. One brother said: 'It is more important to satisfy the needs of the body than to earn a good reputation.' The second brother said: 'It is more important to have a good reputation than to satisfy the needs of the body.' The third brother said: 'A good reputation and the needs of the body are equally important.' So they went to Yang Chu, and said: 'Tell us which of our views is right, and which are wrong.'

Yang Chu replied: 'There was once a man who lived by a wide river. He was an excellent swimmer, and also a skilled boatman. One day a group of people from a nearby city came to the river, and asked him to teach them how to swim. He asked them to board his boat, and he rowed them out into the middle of the river; then he ordered them to dive into the water. Half the people drowned, and half learnt to swim. Which of them were right, and which were wrong?'

The brothers went away, and never argued again.

8

A white and a black coat

A man called Pu put on a white silk coat, and went to visit a friend. While he was at the friend's house, rain began to fall; and when it was time for Pu to return home, rain was still falling. So his friend lent him a black coat that was waterproof; and Pu put his white coat in a bag.

When Pu arrived home, his dog did not recognize him, and barked loudly. Pu was irritated by the noise, and started to beat the dog with a stick. At that moment Yang Chu happened to pass by, and called out: 'Stop beating that dog.' Pu now threatened Yang Chu with his stick. Yang Chu remained calm, and asked Pu why the dog was barking. Pu replied: 'It's barking because it's stupid. I went out in a white coat and returned in a black coat – and it can't recognize me.'

Yang Chu said: 'You are no different yourself. If your dog went for a walk with white hair, and returned with black hair, would you recognize it?' Pu put down his stick, took off the black coat, and put on the white one again. The dog fell silent, and wagged its tail.

8

Good works

Yang Chu said to his disciples: 'If you strive to do good, without any expectation of reward, you may win a high reputation. If you have a high reputation, you may be offered a high office. If you have a high office, you may accumulate great wealth. If you have great wealth, many will try to cheat you, many will try to steal from you, and many will beg from you. So do not strive to do good; simply do whatever good comes naturally to you.'

8

The secret

There was a teacher who claimed to know the secret of immortality. Many people came to him, and asked him the secret. He demanded ten gold coins, and then told them some meaningless nonsense. If they subsequently died, he said that they had failed to understand the secret.

The king heard about this teacher, and sent a messenger to fetch him. The messenger dawdled on the journey; and by the time he reached the teacher's house, the teacher had died. The messenger returned to the palace in great fear. He told the king that he had dawdled, and that in the meantime the teacher had died. The king flew into a rage, and sentenced the messenger to death.

Yang Chu heard about the messenger's plight, and rushed to the palace. He said to the king: 'Your messenger was wrong to dawdle, but you were wrong to send him. The death of the teacher proves that he didn't possess the secret of immortality – otherwise he would still be alive. The secret is that no such secret exists; only a fool would believe otherwise.'

The king released the messenger; and from that moment was happy to face death whenever it came.

8

Brilliance at mathematics

Yang Chu said to his disciples: 'There are many people who possess theories about life, but cannot act on those theories. It is better to act without possessing a theory.

'There was a man who was renowned throughout the world for his brilliance at mathematics. He developed mathematical theories, which he then applied in many practical ways. He thus invented many machines, and then sold them. In this way he grew immensely rich.

'When he was dying, he passed on to his son all his mathematical theories: over several days he explained his theories, and his son memorized them. After the man died, his son found that he could not apply the theories – so they were useless to him.

'A little while later someone called on him, and asked him about his father's mathematical theories. The son related the theories in the exact words that his father had used. The other man went away, and worked out how to apply them. He too became renowned throughout the world for his mathematical brilliance – and he too became immensely rich.'

8

A gesture of kindness

Every new year, as dawn broke, the king released thousands of white doves into the air.

But people throughout the capital city and surrounding countryside chased these doves; and when the doves perched on trees, they tried to catch them in nets. They then kept them as pets in tiny cages.

Yang Chu hated to see these doves in cages, because it was their nature to fly freely. He went to the king, and asked: 'Why do you release these white doves at new year?' 'As a gesture of kindness,' the king replied. Yang Chu said: 'Your gesture of kindness is an act of cruelty.' And he described to the king the fate of the doves.

The king was shocked, and never again released doves. And from that moment onwards he became wary of any kind of gesture.

8

A wise boy

A nobleman was about to go on a long journey. He held a huge banquet on the last evening before the journey. A thousand guests came, and fish and geese were served to them. At the end of the meal the nobleman rose to make a speech. His first words were: 'I wish to thank God for providing fish and geese for human beings to enjoy.' All the guests nodded in agreement.

But a twelve-year-old boy called out: 'You are wrong, sir!' The nobleman was astonished, and asked: 'What do you mean?' The boy said: 'Fish and geese, and all the other living beings on this earth, are born just as humans are born, and die just as humans die. No type of living being is nobler or more worthy than any other; the only difference is that living beings with more strength or intelligence are able to eat those with less strength or intelligence. So it is absurd to say that fish and geese exist for our benefit; we are merely strong and intelligent enough to catch and kill them. Mosquitoes and gnats bite our skin, and tigers and wolves eat our flesh. But do we exist for the benefit of mosquitoes and gnats, tigers and wolves?'

Yang Chu, who was one of the guests, rose up and clapped. Then he declared: 'One child possesses more wisdom than a thousand adults.'

8

An unlucky tree

A man had a tree in his garden. The garden was so small that the tree dominated it. One day his neighbour said to him: 'That type of tree is unlucky. You should chop it down.' So the man chopped it down, and then cut it into logs for firewood. But there were so many logs that they covered all the flowers in his garden. His neighbour said: 'Let me take half the logs, so you can see your flowers again.'

A few days later the man thought: 'Perhaps my tree was not unlucky after all; my neighbour deceived me in order to get firewood for himself.' So he went to Yang Chu, and asked his opinion. Yang Chu smiled, and said: 'The tree was indeed unlucky, as your neighbour said; it is now being burned. Its bad luck was to be owned by a fool.' The man began to weep. Yang Chu added: 'But now you are no longer a fool; you have lost a tree, but gained a valuable lesson. Never again will you take advice, unless you first understand and agree with it.'

8

A lost axe

Yang Chu said to his disciples: 'A man lost an axe. He suspected that a boy, who lived nearby, had stolen it. Whenever he saw the boy, he became more convinced of his guilt. His facial expression, his manner of speaking, and his demeanour seemed, in the man's view, to exude guilt.

'Then a few days later the man found the axe in a corner of his own house. He realized that he must have left it there one evening, and then forgotten about it. Later that day he saw the boy whom he had suspected of theft. Nothing in his facial expression, his manner of speaking or his demeanour suggested guilt.'

Yang Chu concluded: 'So if you wish to discern the truth, ensure that your mind is open.'

8

A blind theft

A certain man earned a modest living as a carpenter. His wife and children were content with what he provided. But he became discontented. He said to himself: 'I am too poor to be happy. If I possessed some gold, then I should be content.'

So one morning he put on his hat and coat, and walked to the market. He went to a goldsmith's stall, and stared at all the gold ornaments. Suddenly he grabbed a gold ornament, and ran off. Several bystanders saw the theft, and gave chase; and they were soon joined by the local constables. They caught up with him, and he was thrown into prison.

Yang Chu went to see him, and asked: 'Why did you steal that gold ornament in front of so many people.' The man replied: 'At that moment I didn't see the people; I just saw the gold.'

Yang Chu then went to see the goldsmith, and said: 'That man is not evil. His heart made him blind; and like any blind person he needs help. I beg you not to press charges against him.' The goldsmith agreed, and the man was released. Yang Chu went to see him at his home every day for a month, and taught his heart to be content with what he had. As a result he could see clearly.

8

KUNG FU TZU

Kung Fu Tzu (Confucius, as he is better known in the West) was born in the middle of the sixth century BCE. His family were poor, but may have been of royal descent. By the age of fifteen he had decided to devote himself to study. His erudition secured him a minor post at court, and he remained in royal service until about the age of fifty. During this time he developed both an ethical and a political philosophy; and he spent the next decade travelling from one kingdom to another, seeking a king who would employ him as advisor. He returned home disappointed. During the last decade of his life he attracted a group of about seventy disciples, and devoted himself to teaching them. His teachings are recorded in *The Analects*.

A flexible mind

It is a pleasure to learn something valuable, and then to apply it. It is a joy to welcome friends who have come from afar. It is virtuous not to take offence when others fail to appreciate your abilities.

Every day I ask myself three questions. Have I served others to the best of my abilities? Have all my words been honest and trustworthy? Have I given advice to others that I do not practice myself?

If you study, and reflect on what you have studied, your mind will become flexible.

You should seek neither a full belly nor a comfortable home. You should be quick in action, but cautious in speech. You should seek the advice of those who follow the Way.

If you are poor, do not flatter the rich. If you are rich, do not despise the poor.

Virtue may be compared with the pole star, which commands the homage of the other stars without ever moving from its place.

At fifteen I set my heart on learning. At thirty I could discern the nature of virtue. At forty I was free from doubts. At fifty I understood destiny. At sixty my ear was attuned to the harmony of all life. At seventy I was free from all evil desires, so no longer needed to control myself.

1.1, 4, 8, 14, 15; 2.1, 4

A missing pin

I have a disciple called Hui. He never disputes or disagrees with what I say. Thus he may seem stupid. But when I examine his behaviour, and when I hear him speaking to others, I understand my own teaching more fully.

Wise people are broadminded, and not partisan; foolish people are partisan, and not broadminded.

If you learn from good teachers, but do not reflect on what they say, then you will become confused. If you reflect deeply, but do not have good teachers to guide you, then you will be in danger.

This is what a king must do to command the respect of the people: he must promote people who are straight, and give them authority over those who are crooked. But if he promotes the crooked, and gives them authority over the straight, he will be despised by the people.

A person may possess numerous virtues; but if honesty is not among them, that person should be avoided. A carriage may be sturdily built, comfortable and elegant; but if the pin is missing from a wheel, it will tip over.

2.9, 14, 15, 19, 22

A beautiful neighbourhood

A town or a village is beautiful if its inhabitants are benevolent. How can people be considered wise, if they do not value benevolence in their neighbours?

Benevolent people are attracted to benevolent people, because they feel comfortable in their company. Wise people are attracted to benevolent people, because they know they will be treated well by them.

If people lack benevolence, how can they win respect? Never abandon benevolence – even for the time it takes to eat a meal.

If a person hears about the Way, and then dies on the same day, that person has not lived in vain.

Do not listen to those who have set their hearts on following the Way, but are ashamed of ragged clothes and simple food.

Do not worry if you do not hold any power; concern yourself only with whether you are worthy of holding power. Do not worry if no one appreciates your wisdom; concern yourself only with whether you are truly wise.

Wise people know what is right. Foolish people know only what is profitable.

4. 1, 2, 5, 8, 9, 14, 16

Water and mountains

A quick and eloquent tongue is a doubtful asset. It frequently provokes resentment and anger in others.

There is no point in condemning people who cannot control their actions. A piece of rotten wood cannot be carved.

When you see that you have made an error, do you take full responsibility? And do you try to change yourself, so that you will not repeat the error? If so, you are very unusual.

A virtuous life is likely to be a long life. Some people without virtue live to a great age; this is because they are lucky. The wise find joy in water, while the benevolent find joy in mountains. The wise are passive, while the benevolent are active.

I do not invent new ideas; I merely transmit old ones. I know that my words are wise, because I repeat the wisdom of ancient sages. These things cause me concern: failure to reflect on what has been learnt about virtue; and failure to apply what has been learnt about virtue.

5.5, 10, 27; 6.19, 23; 7.1, 3,

The cloak and the stick

I have set my heart on following the Way. I have put on the cloak of virtue; I have benevolence as my stick; and I relax by enjoying the arts.

You learn the truth unless the quest for truth has already driven you to distraction. You cannot teach the truth unless the quest to express the truth in words has already put you in a frenzy.

When eating in the presence of the bereaved, do not eat your fill.

You can derive just as much joy from eating coarse rice as eating fine rice, from drinking water as drinking wine, and from resting on a mat as resting on a bed. The joy comes from knowing that you have earned your food, drink and rest by honest means.

You can learn from the company of bad people as well as good people. In good people you see points that you should copy; in bad people you see points on which you should correct yourself.

To be extravagant is to draw attention to yourself; to be frugal is to be ignored. I should rather be ignored than draw attention to myself.

Wise people are confident in themselves; foolish people are anxious about themselves.

7.6, 8, 9, 16, 22, 36, 37

Hammering a question

You may be wise; but less wise people may still enlighten you on certain points. You may be intelligent; but less intelligent people may still have insights that you lack. You may be virtuous; but less virtuous people may still guide you in particular ways.

Most people study in order to earn a higher salary. But it is better to study in order to become wise.

If you devote your life to acquiring wisdom, you will have a good death.

When the king is following the Way, support him; if he offers you a salary as an advisor, give advice and accept the salary. When the king is not following the Way, avoid him; if he offers you a salary as an advisor, give advice and refuse the salary.

I cannot understand people who are ignorant, and yet are impulsive; who lack ability, and yet do not seek help from others.

A man with no education put a question to me, and I could not give an answer. I kept hammering at both sides of the question, and it would not break apart. I thanked the man for exposing my ignorance.

We should hold young people in the highest respect. How do we know whether the next generation will be wiser or more foolish than the present generation? Only when people have reached the age of forty or fifty is it possible to assess them.

8.5, 12, 13, 16; 9.8, 23

Partners for different purposes

When someone speaks with wisdom, you naturally give assent; but assent is worthless unless your attitudes are changed by that wisdom. When someone speaks with insight, you naturally agree; but agreement is worthless unless your behaviour is altered by that insight.

The person of wisdom is never in two minds; the person of benevolence is never indecisive; the person of valour is never afraid.

You may have a friend who is a good partner in your studies; but do not assume that the same person is a good partner in following the Way. You may have a friend who is a good partner in following the Way; but do not assume that the same person is a good partner in opposing evil. You may have a friend who is a good partner in opposing evil; but do not assume that the same person is a good partner in making moral judgements.

When you visit a strange place, behave with humility, as if you yourself were receiving an important guest. When employing another person, behave with respect, as if that person held high office.

Do not impose on others what you would not desire for yourself.

9.24, 29, 30; 12.2

The marks of virtue

The mark of benevolent people is that they are reluctant to speak. They know that benevolent actions are hard; and they do not want to advocate a course of action that they themselves could not follow.

The mark of wise people is that they are free from anxiety. They know how they should live, and they live as they know; so they have no cause for anxiety.

The mark of shrewd people is that their opinion of another person is not influenced by gossip and slander against that person; and their opinion of themselves is not influenced by gossip and slander against themselves.

The mark of gentle people is that they do not feel resentment, and do not hold grudges against those who have wronged them.

If I were to hear that someone was suing me, I should react as any person would. But if I hear that one person is suing another, I intervene, and urge them to settle their differences amicably.

Do not become weary with your daily routine. And when there is action to be taken, give of your best.

Help others to discover their own abilities and virtues; help them find the goodness within their own souls. Help them to suppress that which is bad within them.

12.3, 4, 6, 8, 13, 14, 16

A good friend

To be benevolent is to love other people. To be wise is to understand other people. To be a good ruler is to give good people authority over bad people.

To be a good friend to others is to advise them according to your wisdom, and to guide them according to your insight – but to say nothing when there is no hope of influencing them. There is no point in being snubbed.

If you employ others, your duty is to encourage them. And the best form of encouragement is to set an example: work with them, and do not slacken.

If you rule others, show leniency towards minor offenders, and promote people according to their ability and virtue.

When somebody asks your advice on some matter, and you are ignorant about that matter, remain silent. When you seek advice, and you are not convinced that the advice is right, do not follow it.

When some course of action has failed, do not pretend that it has succeeded.

When a ruler is unjust, so that punishments do not fit crimes, people will not know how they should behave.

12.22, 23; 13.1, 3

Good words and bad words

If you are in a position of authority, and you set a good example to those beneath you, then you will not need to issue orders; when they perceive what you want, they will act immediately. But if you do not set a good example, even your strictest orders will be defied.

If you become wealthy, do not become unduly excited about the fruits of your wealth. A house is only a house, whether it is a mansion or a cottage. Food is only food, whether it is a banquet or a simple meal.

If someone employs you, take time to learn the job. You should aim after a year to be working satisfactorily; and after three years you should be working well.

If a king is benevolent, it takes a generation for his kingdom to become more benevolent.

It is difficult to be a ruler, and it is not easy to be a subject. If a ruler understands the difficulties of being a ruler, he will eventually bring peace and prosperity to his subjects.

The only pleasure of being a ruler is that no one goes against what he says. If his words are good, then all will be well. But if his words are bad, he will bring his kingdom to ruin.

A good ruler pleases those who are near, and attracts those who are far away.

13.6, 8, 11, 12, 15, 16

Petty gains and the larger purpose

In your work do not be impatient. If you are impatient, you will strive after petty gains, and lose sight of the larger purpose.

If your son has committed a crime, there is no virtue in handing him over to the authorities for punishment. Your duty is to protect him from punishment, and to dissuade him from committing further crimes.

Treat those set above you, and those below you, with equal respect; serve all people to the best of your ability.

Cultivate within yourself a sense of shame. Reflect on actions that are wrong; and stir up within yourself a sense of revulsion towards them.

If you have promised to perform some action, then you should generally keep that promise. But if in the course of doing so you realize that the action is wrong, desist at once.

Wise people are able to agree with others without echoing them. Foolish people are able to echo others without agreeing with them.

If you are virtuous, people of virtue will like you. But do not be upset if people without virtue dislike you.

13.17, 18, 19, 20, 23, 24

To serve and to please

Wise people are easy to serve, but difficult to please; you can only please them by following the Way. Foolish people are difficult to serve, but easy to please; you can please them by doing everything they want.

Wise people are comfortable in the company of those with power, wealth and status; they feel no need to assert themselves. Foolish people are uncomfortable in the company of those with power, wealth and status; they constantly feel the need to assert themselves.

Wise people are able to combine eagerness with gentleness, courage with kindness, determination with generosity.

Wise people never ask others to do tasks they would not be willing to perform themselves.

Do not make a salary the sole object of your work. In all activities your primary purpose is to follow the Way.

When someone is in your power, resist the temptation to use that power to your own advantage. When you have performed some noble act, resist the temptation to brag about it. When someone has wronged you, resist the temptation to hold a grudge. When someone is honoured more highly than you, resist the temptation to be envious. Resisting these temptations is hard, but is essential for benevolence.

13.25, 26, 28, 30; 14.1

A complete person

People of virtue say many memorable things; but those who say memorable things, are not necessarily virtuous. Benevolent people possess courage; but those with courage are not necessarily benevolent.

There may be wise people who are not benevolent. But foolish people are never benevolent.

If you are poor, it is difficult not to complain of injustice. But if you are rich, it is even more difficult not to be arrogant.

If you possess wisdom, are free from selfish desires, are courageous, and appreciate music and the other arts, you are a complete person. But a complete person does not need to have all these qualities. If you prefer virtue to profit, and remain virtuous even when poverty befalls you, then you are a complete person.

Speak only when it is time to speak, so people never grow tired of hearing you. Laugh only when there is real humour, so people will laugh with you. Eat only when it is time to eat, so you eat the right amount.

If you lack modesty, you will make claims about yourself that you cannot fulfil.

If you are employed by a man of power, be honest with him. Even when he is annoyed by your words, never cease to be truthful. Then you will render him true service.

14.4, 6, 10, 12, 13, 20, 22

Reasons for study

Wise people study in order to improve themselves; foolish people study in order to impress others.

I constantly seek to reduce the number of errors I make. But I shall never eliminate all errors.

Wise people are afraid of their words outstripping their deeds.

You should not be worried about the failure of others to appreciate your abilities. Your only concern should be to use your abilities in the service of others.

Do not presume that people are deceitful and dishonest. But be quick to spot dishonesty and deceit when they occur.

It is sometimes said that you should repay an injury with a good turn. It is wiser to repay an injury with honesty. Only a good turn should be repaid with a good turn.

In my studies I always start with what is simple and easy, and only gradually move to what is complex and hard.

It is best to detach yourself from the world. If you cannot do that, detach yourself from particular places. If you cannot do that, detach yourself from hostile emotions. If you cannot do that, detach yourself from hostile actions and words.

14.24, 25, 27, 30, 31, 34, 35, 37

The life of pests

Let me describe the life of pests. When they are young, they are neither modest nor respectful. When they have grown up, they do nothing useful for others. And when they are old, they refuse to die.

If young people are eager to be seen among their seniors, and to be treated as equals by their seniors, they will not make progress.

When wise people fall into poverty, and are beset by grave difficulties, they cling onto virtue. But foolish people are quick to cast aside virtue in hard times.

In the course of my life I have learnt many things; and since I have a good memory, I can remember what I have learnt. But I cannot find a common thread that binds all things together.

The greatest rulers achieve order without taking any action.

If your words are honest and your deeds are kind, then even your enemies will respect you. But if your words are often false and your deeds often harsh, even your friends will despise you.

When those around you are following the Way, it is easy to be honest and kind. The hardest challenge is to remain honest and kind even when those around you have abandoned the Way.

14.43, 44; 15.2, 3, 5, 6, 7

Sharp tools

If someone is capable of benefiting from your words, silence would be wasted. If someone is not capable of benefiting from your words, then words would be wasted.

Sometimes benevolence requires people to risk their lives. Do not cling onto life at the expense of benevolence.

Carpenters, before they start a task, have to sharpen their tools. Teachers, before they start teaching, should sharpen their eloquence by learning how their pupils think.

The future approaches with great speed. So if you give no thought to difficulties in the future, you will soon be overwhelmed.

Set strict standards for yourself, but make allowances for others; then you will not incur ill will.

I have known many people who constantly cry: 'What am I to do? What am I to do?' Nothing can be done to help them.

Some groups of friends merely enjoy making witty conversation, without ever touching on moral issues. I can think of nothing duller.

If religious rituals convey moral truth, then participate in them.

15.8, 9, 10, 12, 15, 16, 17, 18

Wise people

Wise people are troubled by their own lack of abilities, not by the failure of others to appreciate those abilities.

Wise people hope to be remembered for what they were; foolish people hope to be remembered for what they did.

Wise people seek goodness within themselves; foolish people seek goodness in others.

Wise people are aware of their own wisdom, but do not treat foolish people with contempt. They like to associate with other wise people, but do not form cliques.

Wise people do not judge the abilities of others by what they say about themselves, but by their actions.

Wise people do not try to impose on others what they do not desire for themselves.

Wise people take pleasure in praising those who deserve praise. But they do not condemn people who deserve condemnation.

People may be educated, and they may be able to write with fluency; but it does not follow that they are wise.

Taking pleasure in your own eloquence, and in your ability to influence others, will undermine your virtue. Lack of self-control will undermine all your plans.

15.19, 20, 21, 22, 23, 24, 25, 26, 27

Fire, water and benevolence

If someone is widely hated, do not assume that the dislike is justified; do not make your own judgement until you have made your own investigation. If someone is widely loved, do not assume that the love is justified; do not make your own judgement until you have made your own investigation.

When you have done wrong, the greater wrong is not to put matters right.

I once spent all night thinking without taking food, and all night thinking without going to bed. But I gained nothing from it.

Wise people regard following the Way as their most important task, and securing food as less important. If you till the soil, and think nothing of the Way, your belly will be full, but your soul empty.

Wise people sometimes make small errors; but taken as a whole their lives are good. Foolish people are sometimes correct; but taken as a whole their lives are bad.

Benevolence is more vital than even fire and water. All three bring great benefits. But people can be burnt to death by fire, and drowned by water, whereas benevolence has never harmed anyone.

Wise people are flexible in small matters, but have firm principles to guide their lives. Foolish people are stubborn in small matters, but have no firm principles to guide their lives.

15.28, 30, 31, 32, 34, 35, 37

Five qualities

In serving your employer you should perform your duties to the best of your ability; your salary is of secondary importance.

Do not strive for eloquence, but speak plainly. Concentrate on conveying your message, not on dazzling your listeners.

All human beings are similar, so they are naturally friendly towards one another. Antipathy and hostility are unnatural.

The most intelligent people are suspicious of change. The least intelligent people are bemused by change. People of ordinary intelligence welcome change.

You use a large knife to chop up an ox; you need only a small knife to chop up a chicken. Use words that are appropriate to each occasion.

Benevolence manifests itself in five qualities: respect for others; tolerance towards others; honesty in speech; promptness in action; and generosity in word and action. If you are respectful, you will not be treated with insolence. If you are tolerant, people will feel comfortable in your presence. If you are honest, you will win people's trust. If you are prompt, you will achieve results. If you are generous, people will love and admire you.

15.38, 41; 17.2, 3, 6

Hard grain and white cloth

Can even the hardest grain withstand grinding? Can even the whitest cloth withstand black dye? If you wish to preserve your virtue, avoid the company of evil people.

Have you heard about the six qualities, and the six faults that may accompany them? To love benevolence, and yet not to love learning, leads to foolishness. To love cleverness, and yet not to love learning, leads to deviousness. To love honesty, and yet not to love learning, leads to crudity. To love resoluteness, and yet not to love learning, leads to intolerance. To love courage, and yet not to love learning, leads to subversion. To love diligence, and yet not to love learning, leads to wasted effort.

Why do you not love poetry? An apt quotation from a poem stimulates the imagination, resolves arguments, and gives tactful expression to complaints.

Why do you not learn the names of birds and animals, plants and trees? By knowing their names you will appreciate them more fully.

Why do you not love to read ancient books of wisdom? To ignore these books is like turning your face towards the wall.

To express love it is not sufficient to offer gifts of jade and silk. To play music it is not sufficient to pluck a lute with skill.

17.7, 8, 9, 10, 11

A coward and a thief

I admire a cowardly person who puts on a brave front. Such a person is like a thief climbing over a wall.

Do not work alongside mean people. Before they get what they want, they worry that they might not get it. When they have got what they want, they worry that they might lose it – and then they will stop at nothing.

Are you wild? If so, you may simply be impatient of restraint; but you are in danger of deviating from the path of virtue. Are you proud? If so, you may simply dislike compromise; but you are in danger of treating others with contempt. Are you foolish? If so, you may simply make many mistakes; but you are in danger of becoming crafty.

It is rare for people with cunning words and ingratiating expressions to be benevolent.

I detest sentimental music for undermining people's appreciation of profound music. I detest cleverness for undermining people's appreciation of wisdom.

If I were to give up speaking, nothing would be lost. Observe the seasons, and watch how life comes and goes; then you will become wise.

If a deceitful person comes to your house, lock the door. Then pick up your lute and start to sing – so the person knows you are home. Thus you will express all that needs to be expressed.

17.12, 15, 16, 17, 18, 19, 20

A full belly and an empty mind

If your belly is always full, you will have difficulty in filling your mind with useful knowledge.

Some people regard courage as the supreme quality. But wise people regard morality as supreme. If people have courage, but are bereft of morality, they become thieves and murderers.

Wise people dislike those who enjoy pointing out the evil in others. They dislike those who slander their superiors. They dislike those whose determination is not tempered by learning. They dislike those who pretend to be wise by quoting the wisdom of others as their own. They dislike those who confuse insolence with courage. They dislike those who confuse exposing the fault of others with honesty.

If you let foolish people grow too close to you, they become insolent. If you keep them at a distance, they complain.

If by the age of forty you have not learnt the art of being likeable, you will never learn it.

When you see an opportunity for profit, do not lose sight of virtue. If you do not hold onto virtue, all your other possessions are useless.

Wise people honour those who are superior to themselves; and they treat with respect those who are inferior. They praise those who are wise, and take pity on those who are foolish.

17.22, 23, 24, 25, 26; 19.1, 2, 3

The workshop and the home

Even minor arts and skills have value. But you should not become proficient in more than a few, for fear that you will be distracted from your larger purpose.

There are two signs that people are eager to learn. The first is awareness of the smallness of their present knowledge. The second is the ability to remember what they already know.

Be broad in your interests, steadfast in your purpose, earnest in your acquisition of knowledge, and reflective about what you know. Then you will not lack benevolence.

Artisans master their trade through staying in the workshop. Teachers acquire wisdom by staying at home.

When foolish people make mistakes, they gloss over them.

When you observe wise people from a distance, they seem formal. When you approach wise people, they seem cordial. When you listen to wise people, they seem firm.

Wise employers try to win the trust of their employers. Only after winning their trust do they set hard and complex tasks – otherwise the employees would feel exploited.

Wise employees try to win the trust of their employees. Only after winning their trust do they offer advice – otherwise the employers would feel slandered.

19.4, 5, 6, 7, 8, 9, 10

Work and study

There is no point in being meticulous in minor matters, if you are careless in major ones.

When you can no longer cope with your job, it may be a sign that you should devote yourself to study. When you find studying dull and dreary, it may be a sign that you should take a job.

When a relative or a friend dies, you begin by mourning; and then mourning turns to grief. When grief is complete, nothing more is required.

A person may be difficult to emulate. But this does not mean that the person has attained benevolence.

If you wish to become benevolent, you need to emulate someone who has attained benevolence. Choose someone whose company you enjoy.

There is only one occasion when every emotion is stretched to the full: when you are mourning the death of a parent.

When you take over a position of power, it is far easier to adopt new policies than to uphold existing policies.

19.11, 12, 13, 14, 15, 16, 17, 18

High office

When wise people make serious errors, it is like an eclipse of the sun or the moon; the whole world seems to darken. When wise people see their errors and correct them, the world becomes light again.

Wise people may be judged foolish by a single foolish word that they utter. Equally foolish people may be judged wise by a single wise word that they utter. So every word counts.

If a wise person helps you to stand, you will stand. If a wise person guides you in some task, you will enjoy success. If a wise person seeks to reconcile enemies, they will see how to resolve their differences. If a wise person sets a group of people a task, they will work in harmony. In life wise people are honoured, and in death they are mourned.

You may have many close relatives. But a few benevolent friends are far more valuable.

To be worthy of holding high office you must be generous, and never count the cost; you must work hard, and never complain; you must be moderate in your desires, and never greedy; you must be intelligent, without being arrogant; you must inspire awe, without being fierce.

You cannot be wise unless you understand destiny. You cannot have principles unless you understand virtue. You cannot judge people unless you understand the meanings of words.

19.21, 25; 20.1, 2, 3

MENG TZU

Meng Tzu (Mencius, as he is better known in the West) was born at the beginning of the fourth century BCE. His teacher had himself studied under Kung Fu Tzu's grandson; and Meng Tzu came to regard himself as Kung Fu Tzu's spiritual heir. He enjoyed debates with other scholars, and he spent forty years travelling from one royal court to another, where he offered his advice. Like Kung Fu Tzu he attracted disciples, who recorded his sayings.

Profit, benevolence and morality

Meng Tzu went to see King Hui. The king said: 'You have come a great distance to see me. You must surely have some way of profiting my kingdom.'

Meng Tzu replied: 'Why must your majesty use the term profit? Benevolence and morality should be your concerns. If you ask only how to profit your kingdom, then your ministers will ask only how to profit their families, and the common people will ask only how to profit themselves. Thus those in both high positions and low positions will be trying to gain at the expense of others, and the entire kingdom will be in danger of collapsing into chaos. Indeed people will soon be plotting to kill you, in the hope of seizing your wealth.

'Just as benevolent people do not turn against their parents, people of morality do not turn against their ruler. That is why I say that benevolence and morality should be your concerns – not profit.'

I.I.I

A sacred garden

A few days later Meng Tzu went to see King Hui again. The king was standing by a pond in his garden, with geese and deer nearby. He asked: 'Is it good and wise to enjoy looking at animals and birds, plants and trees, fish and insects?' Meng Tzu replied: 'You cannot enjoy them unless you are good and wise.'

Meng Tzu continued: 'Long ago there was a king who laid out a beautiful garden, with a lake in the centre. He filled the garden with birds and animals, and the lake with fish and turtles. Every morning he walked round the garden, and derived great pleasure from observing every living being within it. Then he decided to open it to the people of his kingdom. They too were delighted, and they called it "the sacred garden". As the king observed the people walking round the garden, his own pleasure was doubled.'

'Tell me more about this king and his people,' King Hui asked. Meng Tzu replied: 'Since the people now shared his enjoyment of the garden, they loved him. And they declared that they were willing to die for him.'

I.1.2

Ample food

On another occasion Meng Tzu said to King Hui: 'If the farmers do not interfere with their crops, there will be more grain than the people can eat. If the fishermen do not use nets with too fine a mesh, there will be more fish and turtles than the people can eat. If people chop down trees only in the middle of winter, there will be more timber than the people can use. With enough grain, fish and timber, young people will be able to support their parents; and when their parents die, they will be able to provide good coffins and ample food for the funeral feast.

'If mulberry trees are planted near every homestead, there will be ample silk for everyone. If chickens and pigs are allowed to breed in their proper season, there will be ample meat for everyone. If able-bodied people work when there is work to be done, no mouths will go hungry.

'As king you must watch over the education which is provided in schools. Ensure that the children are taught to treat the elderly with respect – so whenever a boy sees someone with grey hairs carrying a load, he will offer to carry that load himself.

'If anyone dies of starvation in your kingdom, you are responsible. Starvation occurs not through lack of food, but because food is not fairly distributed. You alone have authority to impose fairness.'

1.1.3

A true king

King Hui said to Meng Tzu: 'When my father was king, this kingdom was second to none in power. But during my reign territory has been lost in war to the east, west and south. I am deeply ashamed of this; and during my time left on earth I wish to wash away my shame. How can I do this?'

Meng Tzu replied: 'A tiny kingdom is sufficient to enable its ruler to be a true king. The true king is benevolent towards his people. He is merciful in punishment, and lenient in taxation. He urges his farmers to plough deeply, and weed promptly. He encourages all his people to use their spare time in study. He teaches young people to treat their elders with respect, and to be honest in word and deed.

'Indeed, your defeats are a sign of your benevolence. When a king is constantly making war on his neighbours, he takes away the young men from the fields; and as a result his people starve. But your dislike of war has ensured that your people have plenty.'

I.I.5

A marble palace

Meng Tzu went to see King Hsuan. The king had built for himself a magnificent palace; every wall and floor was covered with white marble. The king greeted Meng Tzu: 'Welcome to my home — which I call the Snow Palace. I am sure that a wise man like you can enjoy its beauty.'

Meng Tzu replied: 'Only a fool would not enjoy its beauty. And only a fool would not share its beauty.' 'What do you mean?' the king asked. Meng Tzu replied: 'If people were to criticize their king for not opening his palace to them, that would be wrong — because it is wrong to criticize those in authority. But if the king were not to share the enjoyment of his palace with the people, that would be equally wrong — because by sharing a pleasure it is doubled. The people take delight in the joy of a king who delights in their joy; and they worry over the troubles of a king who worries over their troubles.'

So King Hsuan invited his people to visit the Snow Palace whenever they wished.

1.2.4

Rules for a ruler

King Hsuan said to Meng Tzu: 'Tell me how a king should rule.' Meng Tzu said: 'A king should take as taxes no more than one part in nine of what people produce. His officials may inspect goods as they cross the borders of his kingdom, but they should charge no tariffs. They may inspect goods that are sold in the market-places, to ensure they are properly measured, but they should charge no levy. They should put fish traps in rivers and lakes, and allow anyone to collect the fish caught in them. When the king punishes a man for a crime, he should ensure that the man's wife and children do not suffer also.'

King Hsuan asked: 'Should a king take special care of certain people?' Meng Tzu replied: 'There are four types of people who are particularly vulnerable: old men without wives; old women without husbands; old people without children; and young children without parents. The king should ensure that these people have food, clothes and shelter.'

1.2.5

Wealth and sex

King Hsuan said to Meng Tzu: 'I have a weakness: I am fond of wealth.' Meng Tzu replied: 'If the people are fond of wealth, they ensure their granaries are full; this means that if you must recruit soldiers to defend your kingdom, they will have ample food. Thus there is no harm in being fond of wealth, so long as you share this fondness with your people.'

The king said: 'I have another weakness: I am fond of sex.' Meng Tzu said: 'If the people are fond of sex, there are no young women pining for a husband, and no young men without a wife. So there is no harm in being fond of sex, so long as you share this fondness with your people.'

1.2.5

Tall trees

King Hsuan asked Meng Tzu: 'Tell me how a kingdom can be firm and stable.' Meng Tzu replied: 'Just as a forest needs tall trees, so a kingdom needs officials who are moral and wise.'

King Hsuan asked: 'When I appoint officials, how can I be sure that they are moral and wise?' Meng Tzu replied: 'When your advisors say that a man is moral and wise, do not be satisfied. When your noblemen say that a man is moral and wise, do not be satisfied. Give that man a task in which his goodness and ability are tested; and only if he passes that test should you appoint him.

'Equally if your advisors and noblemen say that a man is amoral and foolish, do not listen to them. Give that man a task in which folly and amorality would be exposed; and if no faults are exposed, appoint him.

'In short, do not believe testimonies about anyone. Believe the evidence of your own eyes.'

1.2.7

A carpenter and an official

Meng Tzu said to King Hsuan: 'If you want to build a mansion, you ask a master carpenter to find huge pieces of timber; and when he has found the timber, you ask him to supervise the construction. He will work to the best of his ability, and the mansion will be fine. But if you were constantly to interfere with his work, and to contradict his decisions, he would soon become demoralized; he would work badly, and the mansion would be unstable and ugly.

'Consider, then, a person who has spent his childhood studying and acquiring knowledge. When he grows up, he naturally wants to put his knowledge to good use. So he comes to you, and asks to work as an official in your service. If you were to entrust him with a particular task, he will work to the best of his ability, and the task will be performed well. But if you were constantly to interfere with his work, and to contradict his decisions, he would soon become demoralized – and the task would be performed badly.'

I.2.9

The people's views

King Hsuan wondered whether to send his army to a neigh-bouring territory, and annex it to his kingdom. So he asked Meng Tzu's advice. Meng Tzu said: 'If you were to annex that territory, would its people be pleased? Would they greet your army with baskets of rice and bottles of wine? Then you should send your army.'

The king sent messengers to the territory to ask the peo-ple their views. The people told the messengers that they would like to be ruled by him. So he sent his army, and an-nexed the territory. The king, who had previously ruled the territory, was angry; and he made an alliance with some other kings to attack King Hsuan. King Hsuan was frightened, and again sought Meng Tzu's advice. Meng Tzu replied: 'A king with the smallest kingdom can conquer an entire em-pire, if his people are with him. A mighty emperor can be defeated if his people are against him.'

King Hsuan was loved by his people. So the young men of his kingdom fought bravely, and defeated the attackers.

1.2.10, 11

A child near a well

Meng Tzu said to his disciples: 'The human soul is naturally sensitive to the sufferings of others. If a king allows his soul to inform his rule, then his government will be compassionate.

'Suppose you were to see a child playing on the edge of the well; you would immediately rush to the well, and pull the child to safety. What would be your motive? Would it be to earn the gratitude of the child's parents? Would it be to win the esteem of neighbours and friends? Would it be because you dislike the sound of a child crying? No, your only motive would be compassion for the child. That is why I say that compassion is natural. Indeed a man or a woman without compassion would not be human.

'Compassion is the seed of benevolence. Shame is the seed of morality. Modesty is the seed of courtesy. And virtue is the seed of wisdom. Human beings have these four seeds in their souls, just as they have four limbs on their bodies. If people break their limbs, they cripple themselves physically; and if they suppress these seeds, they cripple themselves spiritually. If people exercise their limbs, they become physically strong; and if people nurture these seeds, they become spiritually strong.'

                                                    2.1.6

Makers of arrows and armour

Meng Tzu said: 'Is the maker of arrows less compassionate than the maker of armour? The maker of arrows enables people to be killed, while the maker of armour enables people to be protected from death. Is the coffin-maker less compassionate than the physician? The coffin-maker enables people to be comfortable after death, while the physician strives to preserve life. You cannot be too careful about your choice of work.

'The worst folly is not to show benevolence, when nothing stands in the way of benevolence. If you are neither benevolent nor wise, and if you are devoid of both courtesy and morality, then you are a slave to your desires. But if you are benevolent, wise, courteous and moral, then you are free under heaven.

'Benevolence is like archery. An archer ensures that his stance is correct, before releasing the arrow; and if he fails to hit the mark, he blames no one but himself.'

2.1.7

Victory in a siege

Meng Tzu said: 'Heaven's favourable weather is less important than the earth's advantageous terrain; and the earth's
advantageous terrain is less important than human unity.

'Consider an army laying siege to a city. If the weather is
favourable, it will be easy for the soldiers to scale the city
walls; but it will also be easy for the city's soldiers to repel
them. If the terrain is advantageous, with many high rocks,
the soldiers will be able to camp in safety, protected from
enemy arrows; but the citizens will be able to slip out of the
city without detection, and collect supplies. Victory will ulti-
mately be determined by which side fights with greatest
courage and determination – and this will be determined by
the sense of unity amongst the soldiers.

'Thus a kingdom is not made secure by the mountains that
surround it, or by the superiority of its arms, but by the attitudes of its people. If the king follows the Way, and the
people imitate him, then not even the mightiest army can defeat them.

2.2.1

Offers of gold

A disciple said to Meng Tzu: 'Recently the king of Chi offered you a hundred gold coins, and you refused. But in the past you have accepted seventy gold coins from the king of Sung, and fifty gold coins from the king of Hsue. Your attitude to gifts seems inconsistent. Can you explain it?'

Meng Tzu replied: 'In Sung I was about to go on a long journey; and travellers usually receive a parting gift. When the king offered me a bag of seventy gold coins, a note was attached which read: "A parting gift." So I accepted the coins. In Hsue I was in danger of attack, and had to employ guards. The king offered fifty gold coins, with a note which read: "To cover the cost of employing guards." So I accepted the coins. But in Chi there was no reason for the gift. To accept a gift without justification is to put oneself under an obligation to the giver, and is thus tantamount to being bought. So I did not accept it.'

2.2.3

The path towards home

Meng Tzu said to his disciples: 'If you win people's hearts, you win their devotion and loyalty. There is a simple way to win people's hearts: do what they want; and do not impose on them what they dislike. If you are benevolent, people will turn to you, just as water flows downwards and animals head for the forest. But if you are malevolent, you will drive people away, just as the otter drives fish to the river bed and the hawk drives birds into the bushes.

'Do not talk to people who have no respect for themselves; and do not talk to people who have no confidence in themselves. The former attack morality; the latter believe themselves incapable of benevolence. Benevolence is a person's true home, and morality is the path that leads towards it. It is sad that some people despise that path, and condemn themselves never to have a home.'

4.1.9, 10

To dance and wave

Meng Tzu said to his disciples: 'The essence of benevolence is serving your parents. The essence of morality is respect for your elder brothers and sisters. The essence of wisdom is to understand benevolence and wisdom, and to grasp them to your heart.

'The essence of religion is inward devotion. The essence of music is the joy that comes from listening to it. When joy arises, it is impossible to suppress. And when you cannot suppress joy, your feet begin to dance and your arms start to wave.'

4.1.27

Ramparts and ditches

Meng Tzu said: 'If you wish to talk about human nature, do not assert theories or principles. Stick to the facts; then the principles governing human nature will make themselves clear. Clever people love to talk about theories and principles, without regard to facts. And as they put their theories into practice, they do great harm to themselves and to others.

'There was once a flood which threatened to overwhelm a town. Clever people put forward various theories as to how the flood could be stopped. But a wise man called Yu observed the water, and watched how it wanted to flow; then with a few ramparts and ditches he guided it from the town to the fields. In the same way you should observe human nature, and watch how it wants to flow; then you can gently guide human nature away from evil and towards benevolence.'

4.2.26

Cups and bowls

Kao said: 'Human nature is like the willow tree, and morality is like a cup or a bowl. To make human beings moral is
like making cups and bowls out of willow.'

Meng Tzu replied: 'Does the nature of the willow tree
allow you to make cups and bowls from it? Or must you
mutilate the willow in order to make cups and bowls? If you
have to mutilate the willow tree to make cups and bowls,
must you mutilate human beings in order to make them
moral? If people were to follow your words, they would
bring disaster on themselves.'

6.1.1

The flow of water

Kao said: 'Human nature is like the water in a lake. If a breach is made on the eastern bank, the water will flow to the east. If a breach is made on the western bank, it will flow to the west. Human nature does not show any preference for either good or bad, just as water does not show any preference for east or west.'

Meng Tzu replied: 'You are certainly right that water does not show any preference for east or west. But does it show the same indifference to high or low? Just as water naturally flows downwards, so humans are naturally good. There is no water that does not flow downwards; there are no human beings that are not good.

'By splashing your hand on water, you can make it shoot upwards; and with a pump and a dam you can take it to the top of a hill, and force it to remain there. In short, you can contrive circumstances that make water behave against its nature. In the same way circumstances can make human beings behave badly.'

6.1.2

White and whiteness

Kao said: 'Nature is that which is innate.'

Meng Tzu asked: 'Is whiteness that which is white?' 'Yes,' Kao replied. Meng Tzu asked: 'Is the whiteness of white feathers the same as the whiteness of white snow? And is the whiteness of white snow the same as the whiteness of white jade?' 'Yes,' Kao replied.

Meng Tzu said: 'In that case is the nature of a dog the same as the nature of an ox? And is the nature of an ox the same as the nature of a human?'

6.1.3

Roast meat

Kao said: 'Love is internal, not external. Morality is external, not internal.' Meng Tzu said: 'Please explain this view.'

Kao pointed to an old man sitting nearby, and said: 'I respect that man for his age, but he does not owe his age to me. I may observe that some object is white, but its whiteness owes nothing to me. In the same way I may say that a particular person is moral; but that person's morality owes nothing to me. That is why I say that morality is external.'

Meng Tzu replied: 'The whiteness of, say, a white tunic is no different from the whiteness of a white horse. But would you respect an old horse for its age, in the way that you respect an old man for his age? And where does morality lie: in being old; or in treating the elderly with respect?'

Kao said: 'I love my younger brother, yet I do not love your younger brother. The difference in my feelings towards my younger brother and yours lies within me; that is why I say that love is internal. As a moral duty I should treat your elderly father with respect, just as I treat my own elderly father with respect. Thus moral duty lies in their age, not in my emotions; that is why I say that morality is external.'

Meng Tzu said: 'My enjoyment of meat roasted by your brother is the same as my enjoyment of meat roasted by my brother. Does that mean that the enjoyment of roast meat is external?'

6.1.4

An uncle and a younger brother

Chi asked Kung: 'Why do you say that morality is internal?'
Kung replied: 'Morality is the outward expression of the respect I have for others – and that respect is internal.'

Chi said: 'Suppose a person in your village is a year older
than your eldest brother. To whom do you give the greater
respect?' 'My brother.' Kung replied. Chi said: 'Suppose that
they both dined at your house. Whom would you serve first?'
Kung replied: 'The older man.' Chi said: 'So while you have
greater respect for one, your actions give greater honour to
the other. This shows that morality is external.'

Kung could give no reply, and went to Meng Tzu for advice. Meng Tzu said: 'Ask Chi whether he has greater respect
for his uncle or his younger brother. Chi will reply that he
has greater respect for his uncle. But if his younger brother
were presiding at a religious service, during the service he
would show greater respect for his younger brother. This
shows that normal respect is internal; but temporary respect,
arising out of particular circumstances, is external.'

Kung went back to Chi, and recounted Meng Tzu's words.
Chi replied: 'The normal respect I show to my uncle, and the
temporary respect I may show to my younger brother, are the
same; there are not two kinds of respect. This shows that respect is external.' Kung said: 'In summer we drink hot water,
and in winter we drink cold water. Does that mean that our
tastes are also external?'

6.1.5

Nature and circumstances

Kung returned to Meng Tzu, said: 'Some people say that human nature is neither good nor bad. Some say that human nature can become good or it can become bad; thus under one king people behave well, while under another king the same people are cruel and dishonest. Some say that certain people are innately good, while other people are innately bad; it is even possible for a father to be naturally good, and his son to be naturally bad. What do you say?'

Meng Tzu replied: 'If people become bad, that is not the fault of their nature. All people naturally feel compassion and shame; all people naturally regard others with respect; all people naturally love goodness and hate evil. Compassion produces benevolence, shame leads to self-control, respect brings wisdom, and love of goodness and hatred of evil are expressed in morality. These qualities are not welded onto a person; they are present in everyone. Circumstances determine whether people seek these qualities within themselves, or whether they ignore them.'

6.1.6

Seeds of barley

Meng Tzu said: 'Nature endows people with quite similar qualities and abilities. The differences between people are determined by what ensnares their souls.

'Consider barley. On a particular day in spring you sow the seeds; and one seed is exactly the same as another. But when you reap the barley in summer, you find that the harvest is better in some parts of the field than in others. The reason is that the soil is richer in some parts than others.

'All people have feet of a similar shape; thus all shoes have the same form. All palates enjoy similar tastes; thus people in one place eat similar food to people in another. All ears hear the same range of sounds; thus music gives pleasure to everyone, apart from the deaf. All eyes have similar standards of beauty and ugliness; thus particular women are admired by all men, apart from the blind.

'Is the human soul the exception? Is one human soul different from another? No, all human souls have the same range of feelings and the same sense of rightness. The sage is simply someone who discerns what is common to every soul. Goodness gives pleasure to the soul, just as meat gives pleasure to the palate.'

6.1.7

A bald hill

Meng Tzu said: 'There was a time when the hill outside the city was covered in trees; and the trees grew so luxuriantly that the entire hill was shaded by their branches and leaves. Then people began to graze their cattle and sheep on the hill, and these animals ate all the young shoots; so no new trees grew. Then people went to the hill to collect firewood, and they lopped off branches. Eventually the hill was bald – as it remains. People now imagine that the hill was always bald. But is it natural for any hill to lack trees?

'Is it natural for any human being to lack morality? If particular people lack morality, it is because their circumstances have compelled them to let it go. They have led lives in which their moral feelings have been lopped off.'

6.1.8

An ancient game

Meng Tzu said: 'Do not be puzzled by the king's lack of wisdom. If a plant is put in the sun for one day, and then exposed to the cold for ten days, it will soon wither. When I see the king, I nurture the shoots of wisdom. But my visits are rare; and as soon as I leave, his foolish officials reappear. Their stupid ideas soon lop off those shoots.

'Consider the ancient game of yi. If you do not give your whole mind to it, you can never master it. Chu is the best player in the country. Imagine two people asking him to teach them. One of these pupils concentrates his mind on the game, and listens carefully to every word Chu utters. The other pupil hears Chu's words, but allows his mind to wander; he watches a bird outside the window, and dreams of shooting it with his bow. Both have the same lessons, but the first pupil will become adept at yi, while the second pupil will remain inept. Is this because the second pupil is less intelligent than the first? Of course not.

6.1.9

Meng Tzu said: 'I like fish and meat; but if I cannot have both, I should rather have meat. I like life and morality; but if I cannot have both, I should rather have morality.

'Life is precious, but I regard morality as more precious than life; for that reason I would not cling to life at all costs. I dread death, but I dread lack of morality more than death; for that reason I would not flee death in all circumstances.

'If you love life above all things, then you will have no scruples about how you preserve it. And if you dread death above all things, then you will have no scruples about escaping dangers. But morality places constraints on what you may do to preserve life and escape danger. I observe that most people act within those constraints; so I conclude that morality is natural.

'All of us need food in order to remain alive; if we do not have food, we soon die. Suppose you encountered a beggar who was starving. If you were to offer him food, he would eagerly take it. But if you were to insult and abuse him as you offered the food, he would refuse it. This shows that people will not preserve life and escape death at all costs.'

6.1.10

A bent finger

Meng Tzu said: 'Benevolence is the strength in our souls, and morality is the road that we must travel. Some people allow themselves to grow weak, and so they stumble; others deliberately stray from the road. How foolish they are! If one of your sheep were to develop some illness, and so fall to the ground, you would try to heal it. If one of your dogs were to stray, you would go in search of it, and bring it back.

'If one of your fingers were to bend double, you would seek a physician who could straighten it. Even if the finger were causing you no pain, and even if it did not impair your abilities, you would be willing to travel a great distance in order to cure it. The reason is that your hands would now be inferior to other people's hands – and you would resent this. You should react in a similar manner if your soul lacks benevolence, and so is inferior to other people's souls: you should seek a sage who can cure it.'

6.1.11–12

Trees in the garden

Meng Tzu said: 'You know how to tend the trees in your garden, to ensure that every tree thrives. But you are ignorant of
how to tend yourself. Does this mean that you love your trees
more than you love yourself. How absurd!

'In fact you love all parts of yourself, and you care for all
parts. You cannot point to a foot or a piece of skin, and de-
clare that you do not love it. But your character is revealed
by the choices you make about yourself. Do you show greater
care for the less important parts, or for the more important
parts?

'Consider a gardener. If he shows greater care for the
common trees, while neglecting the valuable trees, he is a bad
gardener. Equally if you show greater care for a finger than
for your shoulder and back, you are muddled. If you care
more for your belly than for your mind, you are a fool.'

6.1.13–14

Ears, eyes and the mind

Kao asked: 'Why are some people greater than others?' Meng Tzu replied: 'Some people show greatest care for the most important parts of themselves; these people are great. Other people show greatest care for less important parts of themselves; these people are not great.'

Kao asked: 'Why are some people guided to show greatest care for the most important parts of themselves, while others are guided to show greatest care for less important parts?' Meng Tzu replied: 'Some people are guided by the eyes and ears, and for this reason make wrong judgements about themselves. Others are guided by their minds, and for this reason make right judgements about themselves.'

6.1.15

Honours from heaven and humans

Meng Tzu said: 'There are honours bestowed by heaven, and there are honours bestowed by human beings. Benevolence, morality, honesty, delight in goodness – these are honours bestowed by heaven. Kingship, nobility, wealth, status – these are honours bestowed by human beings.

'Wise people strive to acquire honours bestowed by heaven; and they are indifferent to human honours. Foolish people strive to acquire human honours; and as soon as they acquire them, they discard honours bestowed by heaven.

'All people have the same desire for honour; and all people have the capacity to be worthy of honour. The difference between one person and another lies in the type of honour being pursued.

'When a person has acquired heavenly honours, all desire for human honours fades away. So that person is free from all envy and ambition.'

6.1.16–17

Archery and carpentry

Meng Tzu said: 'Benevolence overcomes cruelty, just as water overcomes fire. But if you practise benevolence today, you are like someone trying to put out a huge bonfire with a cup of water. This does not disprove the capacity of water to overcome fire; it simply shows that the amount of water must be proportionate to the size of the fire.'

On another occasion Meng Tzu said: 'When you wish to learn archery, you watch how an accomplished archer draws the bow – and then you imitate that action. When you wish to learn carpentry, you watch how a master carpenter uses his compass and square – and then you imitate him. Equally, if you wish to learn benevolence, watch a benevolent person – and imitate what you observe.'

6.1.18, 20

Seek and find

Meng Tzu said: 'If you discern your own soul, then you understand your nature; and if you understand your nature, you know heaven. If you respect your soul, and if you give full expression to your nature, you serve heaven. It does not matter whether you are destined to die young or to live into old age. All that matters is your soul and your nature.

'Nothing happens that is not destined to happen; so accept your destiny willingly. If you do not accept your destiny, you are like someone standing next to a wall that is about to collapse. By accepting your destiny, and by following the Way, you will live freely and die peacefully.

'Seek the Way, and you will find it. Abandon the Way, and you will lose it.

'There is no greater joy than to know that you are true to yourself. If you know yourself, and treat others as you would wish them to treat you, then you are following the Way.'

7.1.1, 2, 4, 5

Natural actions, knowledge and feelings

Meng Tzu said: 'Benevolent words do not have such a profound effect on people as benevolent music. Good government does not help people so much as good education. Kings practising good government are feared by people; teachers offering good education are loved by people. Good government enables people to be prosperous; good education enables people to be content.

'If you can do something without having to learn it, that action is natural to you. If you know something without having to reflect on it, that knowledge is natural to you. If you feel something without having to understand it, that feeling is natural to you. All children love their parents, and, as they grow up, they respect their elder brothers; so the actions, knowledge and feelings of love and respect are natural to all human beings.

'Do not do what no one else chooses to do; do not desire what others do not desire.

'It is often said that people acquire virtue, wisdom and skill through adversity. Thus an estranged daughter, or the son of a concubine, have greater virtue, wisdom and skill than those who grew up in normal families.'

7.1.14, 15, 17, 18

A bowl of soup

Meng Tzu said: 'Carpenters and carriage-makers can pass on to others the rules of their craft; but they cannot make them skilful.

'If you do not follow the Way yourself, you cannot expect your children to follow it. If your commands are not in accordance with the Way, you should not expect your children to obey them.

'If you seize every opportunity to do good, you will always have friends. If you equip yourself with every virtue, you will never be led astray.

'A rich man, who is eager for respect, is happy to make large and conspicuous gifts. But when a beggar asks for a bowl of soup, reluctance is written all over the rich man's face.

'Human beings are naturally benevolent; benevolence is the essence of being human. If you understand this, then you understand the Way.'

7.2.5, 9, 10, 11, 16

Beautiful and true

Meng Tzu said: 'The mouth discerns tastes, the eye discerns colours, the ear discerns sounds, the nose discerns smells, and the skin discerns textures. The soul discerns the feelings of others – and this engenders benevolence towards others.

'If you desire something, you call it good. If you admire something, you call it beautiful. If you love something, you call it true. Wisdom is good, beautiful and true. So desire it, admire it, and love it.

'There are things that you cannot bear to see and understand; benevolence consists in extending your range of understanding. There are things that you are not willing to do; morality consists in extending your range of good actions. There are traits in others that you hate; tolerance consists in reducing your range of hatreds.

'Good words may only be heard by one person, but they soon reach far. Good actions may bring benefit to only one person, but they have many consequences.'

7.2.24, 25, 31, 32

BIBLIOGRAPHY

There are a number of translations of the works represented in the present volume. These are the most accessible.

Chuang Tzu, *Basic Writings*, tr. Burton Watson (New York, Columbia University Press, 1964).

Chuang Tzu, *The Inner Chapters*, tr. A.C. Graham (London, George Allen & Unwin, 1981).

Chuang Tzu, *The Book of Chuang Tzu*, tr. Martin Palmer and Elizabeth Breuilly (London and New York, Viking Penguin, 1996).

Confucius, *The Analects*, tr. D.C. Lau (London and New York, Viking Penguin, 1979).

Confucius, *The Analects*, tr. Arthur Waley (London, George Allen & Unwin, 1938, and New York, Random House, 1966).

Lao Tzu, *Tao Te Ching*, tr. D.C. Lau (London and New York, Viking Penguin, 1963).

Lao Tzu, *Tao Te Ching*, tr. Ursula Le Guin (Boston and London, Shambala, 1998).

Lieh Tzu, *The Book of Lieh Tzu*, tr. A.C. Graham (New York, Columbia University Press, 1990).

Meng Tzu, *The Book of Mencius*, tr. D.C. Lau (London and New York, Viking Penguin, 1970).

Yang Chu, *The Garden of Pleasure*, tr. Anton Forke (London, John Murray, 1912).

The illustrations in this volume have been taken from Dubose, Hampden C., *Dragon, Image and Demon* (London, S.W. Partridge, 1886).

INDEX OF WRITERS